Working With Students in Community Colleges

ACPA Publications

Denise Collins, Indiana State University, Books and Media Editor
Karen Haley, Portland State University, Developmental Editor

ACPA–College Student Educators International, headquartered in Washington, DC, at the National Center for Higher Education, is the leading comprehensive student affairs association providing outreach, advocacy, research, and professional development to foster college student learning.

ACPA is committed to publishing materials that are of timely assistance to student affairs practitioners in specific functional areas or topics of concern. ACPA Publications reviews proposals for thought papers, guidance for good practice, handbooks for functional areas, and other guidebooks of demonstrated interest to student affairs practitioners. ACPA Publications welcomes submissions from authors who desire to develop a work to be issued by a national professional association with international interests. Publications are focused subjects that are of immediate and continuing use to the student affairs practitioner.

ACPA continues to be recognized for its leadership in addressing issues and trends in student affairs within higher education. One aspect of our mission is to support and foster college student learning through the generation and dissemination of knowledge, which informs policies, practices, and programs for student affairs professionals and the higher education community through publications. Manuscripts selected for publication are peer-reviewed and professionally edited.

We value feedback regarding this publication and other ACPA products. To find out more, visit www.myacpa.org, e-mail info@acpa.nche.edu, or call 1-202-835-2272.

Working With Students in Community Colleges

Contemporary Strategies for Bridging Theory, Research, and Practice

Edited by

LISA S. KELSAY and
EBONI M. ZAMANI-GALLAHER

Foreword by Susan Salvador
Afterword by Stephanie R. Bulger

College Student
Educators International

STERLING, VIRGINIA

Published by Stylus Publishing, LLC
22883 Quicksilver Drive
Sterling, Virginia 20166-2102

Library of Congress Cataloging-in-Publication Data

Working with students in community colleges : contemporary strategies for
bridging theory, research, and practice / edited by Lisa S. Kelsay and Eboni
M. Zamani-Gallaher ; foreword by Susan Salvador ; Afterword by Stephanie
R. Bulger. — First edition.
    pages cm
Includes bibliographical references and index.
ISBN 978-1-57922-915-3 (cloth : alk. paper)—
ISBN 978-1-57922-916-0 (pbk. : alk. paper)—
ISBN 978-1-57922-917-7 (library networkable e-edition)—
ISBN 978-1-57922-918-4 (consumer e-edition)—
1. Community colleges—United States. 2. Community colleges—United
States—Administration. 3. Community college students—United States.
4. Student affairs services—United States.

LB2328.15.U6W67 2014
378.1'5430973--dc23
                                                      2013049677

13-digit ISBN: 978-1-57922-915-3 (cloth)
13-digit ISBN: 978-1-57922-916-0 (paper)
13-digit ISBN: 978-1-57922-917-7 (library networkable e-edition)
13-digit ISBN: 978-1-57922-918-4 (consumer e-edition)

Printed in the United States of America

All first editions printed on acid-free paper
that meets the American National Standards Institute
Z39-48 Standard.

Bulk Purchases

Quantity discounts are available for use in workshops and for staff
development.
Call 1-800-232-0223

First Edition, 2014

10   9   8   7   6   5   4   3   2   1

I dedicate this work to my parents, Ralph and Penny Kelsay, who always encouraged me to follow my dreams and pursue an education and career that is a great fit for me. Thank you for always believing in me.

—*L.S.K.*

I dedicate this work to my mentors, Bem P. Allen, Debra D. Bragg, and M. Christopher Brown II. You encouraged my aspirations, challenged my thinking, and inspired my call to contribute to the development of students. Thank you for investing in my personal and professional growth.

—*E.M.Z.G.*

Contents

Acknowledgments

THIS BOOK WOULD NOT HAVE BEEN POSSIBLE without the input and support of ACPA–College Student Educators International members as well as the support of our family and friends who have lived with us for the past couple of years while we ruminated pursuing this project. Hence, we share our gratitude for their encouragement along the way.

We would like to thank the ACPA members who participated in the brainstorming session during the 2010 ACPA Convention Commission Open Business Meeting, which inspired creative ideas and served as a springboard for bringing this book to fruition. We would like to express appreciation to the ACPA Commission for Two-Year Colleges for endorsing this endeavor. We are also grateful to have a wonderful slate of practitioner scholars featured in this text who promote student development in theory and in practice.

This book also would not have been possible without support from the ACPA Books and Media Board and especially from Karen Haley. Thank you for all the tips, advice, and support through the process of creating this book.

Finally, we must express thanks to the many peer reviewers who provided critical feedback to the chapter authors. Their insights were outstanding and helpful to our contributors.

PEER REVIEWERS

David Asencio, Broward College
Nancy Bentley, Benedictine University
Shammah Bermudez, Delaware County Community College
Michelle Dykes-Anderson, Kentucky Community & Technical College
    System
Peter A. Fagan, Corning Community College

Norah Fisher, University of Washington
Layla Goushey, St. Louis Community College
Marini Lee, Escuela Avancemos Academy
Alyssa Mittleider, Iowa State University
James M. Mohr, Community Colleges of Spokane
Jeannette M. Passmore, Owens Community College
Danny Pham, Bellevue College
Laura Talbot, South Texas College
Calley Stevens Taylor, Reading Area Community College
Franklyn Taylor, Northern Arizona University
Ben Weihrauch, Community College of Denver
Julie White, Monroe Community College

Foreword

S INCE THEIR BEGINNING in the early 1900s, community colleges have become an important mainstay of American higher education. Today, the nation's community colleges are working to strengthen the American economy and citizenry. Together, they serve increasingly diverse student bodies that comprise nearly half of the undergraduates in the country. These unique institutions provide an environment in which individuals have opportunities to work toward their dreams and goals.

President Barack Obama's focus on community colleges as part of his 2020 College Completion Goal emphasized the need to reexamine institutional practices, philosophies, and theories to best serve students. In April 2012 the American Association of Community Colleges released *Reclaiming the American Dream: Community Colleges and the Nation's Future* (21st Century Commission on the Future of Community College, 2012), providing recommendations for revamping and refining our nation's community college system. The report underscores the need for community colleges to keep focused on their significant mission of access while evolving to address contemporary needs and demands.

In light of these developments, it is clear that this book, *Working With Students in Community Colleges: Contemporary Strategies for Bridging Theory, Research, and Practice*, could not have come at a better time. Lisa S. Kelsay and Eboni M. Zamani-Gallaher have gathered a discerning and useful compilation that addresses student cohorts, college readiness, technology, institutional trends, partnerships, and student development theories and related research. The resulting work provides insightful strategies and recommendations for strengthening services and targeting internal and external barriers for change and partnerships. It is a valuable resource that will help readers understand community colleges and the needs and characteristics of their students as well as help to gauge how agile and responsive these colleges are to demands and changes.

The authors of the book's chapters represent higher education practitioners, graduate students, researchers, and faculty members. From their different perspectives, these stakeholders in the field provide insight, history, advice, research, theories, predictions, challenges, and recommendations. The book begins with an overview of community colleges' histories, illustrating how these institutions have responded over the years to the multitude of growing community needs and putting into perspective the institutions' future roles as their communities' colleges. The text also examines the diverse nature of community college student bodies and the impact on the colleges' operations and priorities.

As community colleges embrace the open-door mission, they are continuously challenged with students entering with various levels of college readiness. The issue of the impact of the open-door mission as well as the resulting need for community colleges to provide services for students with multiple needs is discussed in this book. However, the gap in college readiness is evident in the technical divide that is very noticeable among community college students. Hence, the book brings into focus the importance of technical skills not only in the competitive workforce but also for students navigating the institution's technology-infused systems. The political and economic climate continuously affects community colleges in supportive and challenging ways. The book critically examines how these two elements affect current and future decisions.

Committed and defined collaboration between student and academic services is paramount to best serve and support students. Without this relationship, efforts are isolated and lack impact. This partnership and its value for student success are explored in detail. Another feature of this text is its vision of community college orientation programs of the future and their importance with new and transfer students. Orientation is purposefully designed for awareness, integration, education, and involvement, and the addition of residence halls to several community colleges provides defined and focused living and learning opportunities for some students. Subsequently, the implications of residence life at community colleges are discussed as well as strategies to work with residence hall student cohorts.

An important group at two-year colleges are student veterans. Institutional practices and support services required to serve this unique population effectively as they readjust to civilian life as community college students are outlined in this book. In addition, many students enrolled at community colleges are women of color. As a subgroup, their needs and experiences do not receive a great deal of attention in the literature. Explorations for leadership engagement that may help or hinder their transfer rate are discussed at length. In addition, there is a growing trend of older adults seeking learning at community colleges. The authors refer to relevant theories and motivating factors shared by mature adult learners in the pursuit of higher education.

The book closes by addressing how concepts of cultural and social capital affect the campus climate for a diverse population of students and provides recommendations for education professionals and community college leaders.

These chapters provide a timely and valuable resource for the array of professionals working to adapt and evolve their practices in an exciting and challenging time for community colleges. The comprehensive treatment of institutional operations and student progress makes this book an important resource for education professionals, administrators, and faculty. In addition, this book provides insightful strategies and recommendations for strengthening student services and identifying internal and external barriers for change and partnerships.

In short, graduate students in college student development and higher education administration programs, which often marginalize discussions, readings, and research regarding community colleges (Katsinas, 1996; Young & Brooks, 2008), would benefit from the work presented in this book. Twenty-five years ago, I began working at Monroe Community College, a large, comprehensive, multicampus institution in Rochester, New York. I immediately fell in love with the mission of community colleges, the diversity of their student body, and the focus these institutions have on their communities' economic and workforce strength and development. It was as clear then as it is now that community colleges share a priority on breaking down economic and social barriers relating to postsecondary education. Those of us who work in the field are continually humbled by the life journeys of the students who are able to pursue their education. It is our responsibility to serve students the best ways we can. Having this book in our toolbox will go a long way toward helping us achieve this goal. I applaud the leadership of ACPA's Commission for Two-Year Colleges for entrusting this important publication to editors Kelsay and Zamani-Gallaher. If you embrace our responsibility to serve the community college student sector effectively, you will turn the pages of this book with the realization that it is a necessary instrument for the community college professional's toolbox.

Susan Salvador
Vice President
Enrollment and Student Affairs
Northampton Community College
Bethlehem, Pennsylvania

REFERENCES

Katsinas, S. G. (1996). Preparing leaders for diverse institutional settings. *New Directions for Community Colleges*, (95), 15–25.

Murray, D. (2009, July 14). *GRCC president says school is ready to increase enrollment, job-training with federal funds promised by Obama*. Retrieved from http://www.mlive.com/politics/index.ssf/2009/07/index_8.html

21st Century Commission on the Future of Community Colleges. (2012). *Reclaiming the American dream: Community colleges and the nation's future*. Retrieved from http://www.aacc.nche.edu/AboutCC/21stcenturyreport/index.html

Young, M. D., & Brooks, S. D. (2008). Supporting graduate students of color in educational administration preparation programs: Faculty perspectives on best practices, possibilities, and problems. *Educational Administration Quarterly*, 44(3), 391–423.

Preface

COMMUNITY COLLEGES have long served as the centers of educational access and opportunity for significant numbers of students from various walks of life. Since their origin, community colleges have been the most inclusive tier of postsecondary education, providing admittance to all segments of society, no matter the level of readiness, goals, or finances. In an effort to bring to light the historical significance and contemporary importance of American community colleges, this volume seeks to disseminate practitioner scholarship on relevant issues facing two-year institutions and the students they serve. This volume assists the reader in understanding how academic and student affairs leaders identify challenges, foster opportunities, and create strategies for promoting student development in community colleges. Moreover, the book blends theory and practice in describing student services, programs, policies, and best practices in community college education.

Working With Students in Community Colleges: Contemporary Strategies for Bridging Theory, Research, and Practice includes contributions representing a range of areas relevant to the effective schooling and overall development of collegians in two-year institutions. There is a marked underrepresentation and arguable invisibility in the literature of divergent student populations and their developmental concerns at community colleges. Placing community college students at the center, this book introduces interdisciplinary conceptual and applied perspectives highlighting the cross section of community college students.

The book has three parts: "Understanding Today's Community College Campuses," "Welcome to Campus: Supporting Today's Community College Learners," and "A Closer Look: Specialized Populations and Communities on Two-Year Campuses." It is our hope that this book is attractive to various higher education and student affairs graduate programs, in addition to community college leadership programs. We also feel this text will appeal to community college units, particularly in student services. The book invites the reader to engage critically in proactive consideration of how best to meet the academic, social, and community needs of students accessing postsecondary education at community colleges. Our central aim is to encourage thoughtful reading, critical thinking, and informed conversations that meld theoretical perspectives, methodological considerations, and practical applications for framing recommended changes in critical matters affecting the student development of collegians in two-year settings. Moreover, it is our hope that this book spurs community college professionals to call into question how they could be increasingly responsive and reflective in meeting the needs of diverse student populations at two-year institutions.

Part One

Understanding Today's Community College Campuses

THE OPENING CHAPTER BY LISA S. KELSAY AND BETSY OUDENHOVEN provides a brief overview of the history of two-year public community colleges using Joliet Junior College, the nation's first continuously operating public community college, as an example of the evolution of the modern comprehensive community college. In addition, they discuss the relationship of two-year institutions to secondary education and their unique contributions to the landscape of higher education (e.g., growth of vocational offerings, strengthening of the access mission, transfer opportunities). As the nation turns its collective attention to these complex institutions, this chapter appropriately revisits the forces that shaped community colleges in the 20th century to illuminate their purpose and potential in the decades ahead.

John L. Jamrogowicz argues in Chapter 2 that public community colleges are not known for their graduation rates, given the open door that provides access to many Americans who may not otherwise have the opportunity to attend college. Jamrogowicz deliberates on the importance of President Barack Obama's 2009 American Graduation Initiative, which was a call to action for higher education and situated

1

community colleges as key partners in fostering global competitiveness by bolstering the number of working Americans with a college degree. This chapter explores the current economic climate and policy landscape in which community colleges operate.

An open-door mission suggests that every student who walks through the door may be accepted and begin a college education. Is every student who walks through that door ready for college courses? What are the challenges and successes of working with an open-door mission? Patricia Munsch, Tania Velazquez, and Corinne Kowpak explore answers to these questions in Chapter 3 and share methods of working with remedial students to increase retention.

The last chapter in this first section, written by Susan J. Procter and Julie Uranis, explores interesting challenges facing the net generation, as high school students are arriving at community colleges with varied levels of technical skills. Although today's community college students are savvy Web 2.0 consumers, their lack of substantive computer skills leaves them unable to use technology in postsecondary academic environments for student tasks such as registration and online bill payment or to use computers to complete academic assignments. This is a major cause of concern for faculty, administrators, and employers. By establishing technology proficiency as a core competency in community college curricula, educational leaders can help students prepare for 21st-century jobs or for advanced academic work. To fulfill this mission, community colleges must have an accurate measure of the technology skills students possess and a clear definition of the technological competencies needed for the future. Methods for assessing technological literacy are discussed as well as suggestions for embedding technological literacy throughout the community college curricula.

1

Junior Grows Up

A Brief History of Community Colleges

Lisa S. Kelsay and Betsy Oudenhoven

HISTORY DIRECTS US, educates us, allows us to learn and grow, and guides us to where we are today. In the community college arena, we have grown up through the years from offering advanced courses in the high schools to offering dual credit options, certificates, and associate's degrees. This chapter discusses how the community college has grown and evolved starting with the dreams of J. Stanley Brown and William Rainey Harper.

THE BEGINNING

The *Charles E. Stuart v. School District No. 1 of the Village of Kalamazoo* case in 1874 pushed the idea of high school education to the forefront of public education and increased high school enrollment 600% over the next 30 years (Witt, Wattenbarger, Gollattscheck, & Suppiger, 1994). With the increase of high school students and graduates, an idea surfaced to develop six-year high schools to include two years of college and build junior colleges to make college more affordable to the everyday citizen (Witt et al., 1994). California was the first state to offer the first two years of college classes for students while they were in high school when legislation was passed in 1907 (Vaughan, 2000). Additional factors over the years that contributed to

3

the growth of community colleges included baby boomers born after World War II, the civil rights movement, and an increased commitment by the federal government to provide additional funds to college students (Vaughan, 2000).

J. Stanley Brown, principal of Joliet High School in Illinois and then superintendent of the Joliet high school district, pushed for advanced courses for students. It appears that Brown's intent was to help his students transfer and complete their baccalaureate degrees (Sterling, 2001). His hard work allowed students to transfer as college juniors from Joliet high schools to area four-year colleges (Witt et al., 1994).

Concurrent with Brown's efforts at Joliet, William Rainey Harper, first president of the University of Chicago, was restructuring the university into what he called an *academic college* for freshmen and sophomores, and a *university college* for juniors and seniors (Beach, 2011; Sterling, 2001; Witt et al., 1994). By 1896 the academic college was called the *junior college*, and its broad course work in the arts and sciences, now referred to as general education, was called *collegiate study* (Sterling, 2001). Harper worked on this restructuring because he believed that

> the work of the freshman and sophomore years is only a continuation of the academy or high school work. It is a continuation, not only of the subject matter studied, but also of the methods employed. It is not until the end of the sophomore year that university methods of instruction may be employed to advantage. (Sterling, 2001, p. 7)

The presidents of the University of Michigan and the University of Minnesota also supported the idea that the first two years of college should be aligned with secondary education. This also appears to be the start of what is now called *dual credit* between high schools and colleges. Professor Francis W. Kelsey from the University of Michigan wrote to J. Stanley Brown,

> I am much pleased to learn that you have taken your students over more than the required preparatory work. If you will kindly give to those who come to the University of Michigan a certificate to the effect that the extra work has been well done, I will see that advanced credit is given to it. (Sterling, 2001, p. 6)

In part because of proximity, fortuitous timing, and convergent interests, by 1899 "the University of Chicago had approved Joliet High School

as a cooperative school and had begun awarding students advanced credit"
(Sterling, 2001, p. 7). What followed was possible partly because of the construction of a new high school, which provided space to expand the existing
postgraduate courses and offer the first two years of college.

> The creation of a new township district in 1899 broadened the tax base suf-
> ficiently to fund the junior college in its infancy, and the building of a new
> high school in 1901 provided modern classrooms and laboratories for teach-
> ing freshman and sophomore-level college classes. (Sterling, 2001, p. 8)

Now recognized as the oldest community college in the nation, in 1900
Joliet Junior College (JJC) was located in a booming city of 30,000 located
50 miles southwest of Chicago (Wood, 1987). In spring 1901 JJC had six
students enrolled in arts and sciences and 25 students enrolled in a normal
course for training elementary teachers (Sterling, 2001), but in general, "the
original community colleges at the turn of the 20th century focused on the
traditional liberal arts education" (Badolato, 2010, para. 9).

While Joliet was leading the way in Illinois, other states were also adopting
and adapting the idea. In Massachusetts, "junior colleges first began as normal
schools" (Ratcliff, n.d., para. 7). Wisconsin and California took the first steps
to creating a community college system. The University of Wisconsin created
the Wisconsin Idea stating, "education should influence people's lives beyond
the boundaries of the classroom" ("The Wisconsin Idea: History of the Wisconsin Idea," 2013, para. 1), and California passed legislation allowing high
schools to offer college-level work. David Starr Jordan, president of Stanford
University, wrote that he was looking forward "to the time when the large
high schools of [California] . . . will relieve the two great universities from the
expense and from the necessity of giving instruction of the first two university
years" (Brint & Karabel, 1989, p. 27). Additional states including Iowa, Kan-
sas, Michigan, Mississippi, Missouri, Oklahoma, and Texas also established
junior colleges in the early 1900s (Vaughan, 2000), many of which exist today.

In 1917 Brown sought accreditation for JJC through the North Central Association of College and Secondary Schools (Sterling, 2001). JJC was
the "first junior college organization to establish accreditation standards for
admissions policies, faculty qualifications, and funding" (Beach, 2011, p. 7),
and in 1918 the college began to award associate's degrees at formal ceremo-
nies (Sterling, 2001). The return of veterans from World War I resulted in
increased enrollment and diversification of the junior college population. In
addition, the population of high school graduates nationwide rose 150%

between 1920 and 1930 (Cohen, 1998). In his comprehensive history of JJC, Sterling noted that by 1927, "the college truly was in a period of transition from narrowly serving academically gifted students to more broadly training students for semi-professional jobs as well" (p. 27). By the early 1930s, programs were offered for transfer and nontransfer students (Sterling, 2001), and in several states occupational placements were offered (Drury, 2003). For example, in California, Pasadena Junior College created relationships with area business leaders, created advisory committees, and hired guidance counselors to assist the students in their training (Drury, 2003).

The inclusion of an occupational/vocational curriculum was also fueled by support from a national organization for junior colleges, originally called the American Association of Junior Colleges and now known as the American Association of Community Colleges (AACC). This organization, formed in 1921, began "as a forum for the nation's two-year colleges" (AACC, 2013, para. 1) and became the voice for the emerging institutions. The founding of *Junior College Journal* in 1930 provided a forum for promoting a vocational curriculum (Brint & Karabel, 1989; Vaughan, 2000).

The introduction of occupational/vocational programs with terminal degrees was a national trend by the 1930s (Beach, 2011); for example, JJC began a nursing program through an agreement with a local hospital. In response to the Great Depression, many colleges added job training to their repertoire to address widespread unemployment. In addition to job training, students also sought to take advantage of junior college courses because they were free of charge to residents. Over time, the government withdrew some of its financial support of the free community college programs and began to charge tuition (Sterling, 2001). In response to charging tuition at these colleges, financial resources were developed for students and included grants, scholarships through private donations, loans, and jobs at nonprofit organizations (Sterling, 2001).

Although not much has been written about the historical evolution of the services or out-of-class activities of these new institutions, Sterling (2001) noted that JJC did have athletics, clubs and organizations, a newspaper (still called *The Blazer*), a yearbook, and a student council. In the 1931 *Joliet Township High School Bulletin*, it was noted that "these extra-curricular activities were without question a factor of considerable importance in the growth of the junior college. Not only did they help crystallize the junior college into an institution, but they went far in arousing a desire or a willingness among high school seniors to do their first years of beginning work in Joliet" (Sterling, 2001, p. 29),

World War II brought about a drop in enrollment as well as changes to the academic schedule to accommodate working students who needed evening and weekend classes. However, with the passage of the GI Bill in 1944 and the end of the war, enrollments surged once again as veterans began to use their educational benefits in record numbers (Vaughan, 2000). JJC enrolled 179 students in 1943 and 700 students by the fall of 1946, half of them veterans (Sterling, 2001). Throughout the country, "by the fall of 1946 nearly 43% of all junior college students were veterans" (Witt et al., 1994, p. 126). In 1947 the Truman Commission's report on higher education ushered in the era of the community college by recognizing the importance of two-year institutions (referred to in the report as "community colleges") in democratizing education and calling on the states to establish two-year public college systems that would offer accessible and affordable education to the public (Vaughan, 2000).

Although the Truman Commission report expanded the scope of these continually evolving institutions, funding remained a challenge. In 1955 Illinois approved sharing state resources with junior colleges and in 1959 established separate junior college districts (Sterling, 2001). At this time, the state also changed the apportionment formula from a flat rate per full-time student to a rate per semester credit hour (Sterling, 2001). Elmer Rowley, dean of JJC in 1947, "believed two-year institutions should receive financial support from the state like four-year colleges and universities did, and that they should exist within their own districts" (Rohder, 2010, p. 23) and worked to make that a reality. In 1965 the Illinois General Assembly passed the Junior College Act, and the college, which had suspended tuition in 1949, began again to require per-credit-hour tuition for in-district students (Lach, 1998; Sterling, 2001). In addition, this act allowed for the governing of Illinois junior or community colleges through the Illinois Board of Higher Education and stated how funding, sites, and classes would be defined (Lach, 1998).

THE 1960s

The most significant expansion of community colleges in their history as well as an accompanying increase in the enrollment of women and minorities took place during the 1960s (Drury, 2003). By the fall of 1970, the United States had about 1,000 community colleges, representing every state, with an enrollment of nearly 2.5 million students (Witt et al., 1994). By the early 1960s, large cities had multiple colleges. According to Witt et al. (1994), "Chicago had 9 junior colleges, Los Angeles had 6, and New York City had 5" (p. 184). However, most colleges were in smaller cities and communities that did not have a university nearby. There are several reasons for the enrollment increase, but the most prevalent one appears to be the return of veterans from the Vietnam War and those "avoiding the military draft" (Witt et al., 1994, p. 185).

Globally, community colleges were growing as well, especially in Canada and Japan. Japan offered two- and three-year programs at junior colleges that started as comprehensive community colleges under "article 109 of the School Education Law, which unfortunately branded them as temporary higher institutions and thus undermined their credibility" (Witt et al., 1994, p. 202). The national Japanese government ran 28 men-only junior colleges, and local Japanese governments ran 25 mixed-sex junior colleges in the 1960s (Witt et al., 1994). Canada also developed two- and three-year-program colleges and had 106 in place by the end of the 1960s (Witt et al., 1994). Countries such as Colombia, Jordan, Sri Lanka, and the Dominican Republic also created community colleges in the 1960s (Witt et al., 1994).

The open-door or open-access mission was central in the community college. The open door allowed high school students, students who had not completed a high school diploma, and those with a high school diploma (traditional or nontraditional aged) to attend class and earn a certificate or degree for the first time (Vaughan, 2000; Witt et al., 1994). Open access is "a manifestation of the belief that a democracy can thrive, indeed survive, only if its people are educated to their fullest potential" (Vaughan, 2000, p. 4) and removes potential barriers to those previously neglected in the higher education system.

With rising enrollments, the cost of running larger colleges with more faculty and students also increased. Unfortunately, the resultant increase in tuition costs decreased access, as many students were unable to pay for classes. The establishment of federal financial aid for community college students was a welcome development in the 1960s. President Lyndon Johnson signed the Higher Education Facilities Act and the Vocational Education Act in 1963, which provided $1.2 billion and $450 million for construction of community college buildings and education (Witt et al., 1994). Loan programs such as the National Defense Student Loan, the Guaranteed Student Loan, and National Vocational Student Loan Insurance provided loans to students pursuing academic and vocational training. With the addition of the Higher Education Act of 1965, the Manpower Development and Training Act of 1962, and the National Defense Education Act of 1958, it was possible for Americans of every socioeconomic status to attend college.

THE 1970s

As JJC entered the 1970s, one of the first orders of business for the relatively new board of trustees (elected for the first time in 1967) was to vote on the name of the college and whether "community" should replace "junior" (Sterling, 2001). Community had become a popular addition to or change in the name of many of the community colleges established in the 1960s. JJC trustee William Glasscock asserted, "When Junior grows up and has gray hair, the neighbors still call him Junior" (Sterling, 2001, p. 133). Therefore, despite the fact that JJC had indeed grown up, *Junior* remained in its title, in large part for its historical significance.

However, community colleges were still trying to find their way and establish credibility with a public at times skeptical of institutions that looked physically more like high schools than college campuses and did not offer the baccalaureate degree. The link with their high school origins remained strong: Teachers at community colleges in the 1970s tended to come from secondary school teaching positions (Cohen, 1998). In addition, not everyone understood, or supported, the open-access mission. The Carnegie Commission on Higher Education (1970) endorsed community colleges with the following caveat:

> The Carnegie Commission supports open access to the "open door" college for all high school graduates and otherwise qualified individuals. The community colleges have a particular role to play in assuring equality of opportunity to all Americans. The Commission, while supporting open access, does not believe that all young people either want higher education or can benefit from it. (p. 2)

Institutional diversity in the two-year college sector was also in evidence. By 1975 there were 1,200 community and junior colleges, only 222 of which were private (Cohen, 1998). The transfer function continued to depend on proximity to senior institutions and the degree to which credits transferred to four-year institutions. In part because of variations by state, some two-year institutions developed a stronger vocational emphasis. In Indiana and North Carolina, the community colleges grew out of technical institutes and vocational training centers. Strong occupational or vocational programs in Pennsylvania, South Carolina, and Wisconsin were the result of a state system that provided two-year branch campuses for prebaccalaureate study as well as separate technical college systems. Kentucky and Hawai'i colleges fell under the university system and offered transfer and occupational or vocational study (Cohen, 1998).

Through the 1960s and into the 1970s, the baby boomers came of age and went to college. By 1970, "Junior college enrollment increased by more than 11%, hitting an all-time record of nearly 2.5 million students" (Witt et al., 1994, p. 230). Researchers questioned the success of these students in achieving their goals. According to Pascarella and Terenzini (2005), "Two-year matriculants who make the transfer are as likely as four-year matriculants to persist overall (76% versus 78%)" (p. 376). However, whether students enrolled in transfer programs actually transfer is the sticking point.

The 1970s also brought a needed change to the curriculum. "The transformation of the community college from a transfer-oriented institution to one emphasizing vocational training is one of the most fundamental changes to have taken place in the history of 20th century American higher education" (Brint & Karabel, 1989, p. 214). On the student affairs side, student services remained largely a loose collection of individual functions. Without a residential component, community colleges had more of a commuter student focus. However, community colleges have always been student-centered institutions, and small classes and initially small institutional enrollments did allow community college faculty and staff to get to know and care for their students.

In addition to the student aid from federal, state, and local sources started in the late 1960s, the first authorization of the Basic Educational Opportunity Grants (Pell Grants) in 1972 widened the door to higher education. A major theme of the Carnegie Commission's (1970) report emphasized the need for financing to be shared by all levels of governments. With the increase of multiple sources of financial assistance to students, student affairs staff not only managed the increasing complexity of aid but also provided all the other student services including advising, counseling, and support services that growing enrollments required.

THE 1980s

Student aid is a necessary component of access for many college students and has been particularly critical for low-income students seeking educational opportunity. In the mid-1970s, 83% of all financial aid and 80% of federal aid came from grants (Cohen, 1998). After the inception of Pell Grants in the 1970s, a shift occurred in the 1980s. By the end of the 1980s, aid from grants at all levels was reduced to 51% and reduced to 61% of grants stemming from federal aid (Cohen, 1998).

There was also a substantial career focus throughout higher education in the 1980s, which reflected the view that education benefited individuals by equipping them to find good jobs. The 1980s became the decade of specialized training and vocational programs (Drury, 2003). In 1984 the Carl D. Perkins Vocational Education Act replaced the Vocational Education Act of 1963 and provided federal assistance for vocational education. "In 1988 the nationwide Committee on the Future of Community Colleges recommended that these colleges help build communities by creating partnerships with employers and making facilities available for workforce training" (Kasper, 2002–2003, p. 16).

By 1980 overall student enrollment rose to 4.3 million (Kasper, 2002–2003), and the growth in minority populations continued to increase. During the 1989–90 academic year, community colleges conferred degrees to 23,108 African American students, 16,341 Hispanic students, and 10,502 Asian and Pacific Islander students (Kasper, 2002–2003). The designation Hispanic-serving institutions was established in 1986 for two-year and four-year institutions with at least 25% Hispanic student enrollment (Hispanic Association of Colleges and Universities, 2013); 18 institutions were designated as Hispanic-serving institutions during that year.

Through the 1980s and into the 1990s, the community colleges built in the 1960s were largely able to accommodate the rise in the number of students who sought to attend college. They were well located, low cost, and able to accommodate a range of individual goals.

THE 1990s

By the 1990s community colleges were complex institutions with multiple missions and extremely diverse student bodies. The majority of these colleges offered prebaccalaureate transfer programs and occupational programs (which became more commonly referred to as *vocational* programs) as well as developmental education, continuing education, adult education, dual credit, English language learning, high school equivalency training, workforce training, and many other programs. In addition, the numbers of full-time and part-time students increased in the 1990s. "Part-time enrollments in community college rose from about 1.1 million in 1970 to more than 3.4 million in 1999, an increase of more than 200%" (Kasper, 2002–2003, p. 20). The 18- to 21-year-old demographic grew from 56% to 61% of the overall student population from 1993 to 1999 (Kasper, 2002–2003) as the number of older, nontraditional-age students decreased.

During this decade certificates in career programs increased; traditional associate's degree programs grew stronger; and the new, primarily technology-related curricula were added. Community colleges positioned themselves to address the demands of a more information-based economy. At the same time, student affairs staff at community colleges began to address issues of student success and their role in providing academic advising, career counseling, and academic support services such as tutoring, services for students with disabilities, and support programs for underrepresented students. As career and technical programs solidified their offerings, the faculty who had launched these programs in the 1960s and who felt personal and professional ownership for their success began to retire. It was common at community colleges for many faculty and staff to stay for 30 or more years; however, with their departure, some institutional history was lost.

States began to formalize relationships with community colleges through statewide articulation initiatives that would ensure ease of transfer from public community colleges to public (and sometimes private) four-year institutions (Cohen, 2001). Thus, while the career and technical programs continued to expand, there were efforts to improve the transfer function of these institutions as well. For example, although articulation of courses between junior colleges and four-year institutions began in Illinois in 1901, it was not until 1998 that the Illinois Articulation Initiative went into effect statewide with the implementation of the widely accepted General Education Core (Illinois Board of Higher Education, 1998).

2000 TO THE PRESENT

In the first half of the 20th century, the United States provided universal access to secondary education, and as we began the 21st century, community colleges provided nearly universal access to college (Rosenbaum, Deil-Amen, & Person, 2006). According to the AACC (2013), as of January 2013 there were 1,132 two-year institutions, 986 of which were public, 115 were independent, and 31 were tribal. The fall 2011 head count for community college students was 13 million, with 8 million in credit classes and 5 million in noncredit classes (AACC, 2013). The average age of students was 28; 57% were women, 43% were minority, 40% were first generation, 41% were full-time, 59% were part-time, and 34% were Pell Grant recipients (AACC, 2013). As these numbers illustrate, community colleges are representative of those who live in the community.

As calls for completion and increased accountability echo throughout higher education, community colleges have a dilemma in how to measure what they do. How does one measure the success of a student who transfers prior to graduation, who retools and finds a job, who learns English, who discovers a new hobby in retirement, or who finally completes high school? As the students and the programs have diversified, so too have the outcomes. However, administrators of community colleges know their measured success rates are not what they should be, especially for low-income students who are most in need of what these institutions have to offer (Fike & Fike, 2008).

At a time of widespread turmoil in the national economy and great concern about reduced levels of state support for higher education, the president of the United States has turned the nation's attention to community colleges for solutions. The Obama administration has focused on community colleges as a critical point of access to higher education and an important component of economic recovery. President Obama has been clear in his expectations, stating, "It's time to reform our community colleges so that they provide Americans of all ages a chance to learn the skills and knowledge necessary to compete for the jobs of the future" (as cited in Badolato, 2010, p. 1). Although attention to and respect for community colleges may be long overdue, being in the national spotlight also raises expectations and increases calls for accountability. Many community college students are successful in reaching their goals and many could not have done so without these institutions. However, the challenge of the coming years will be in trying to find ways to help *more* students meet their educational goals, find sustaining and satisfying work, and become contributing members of society.

Many community colleges have once again reached back and formed partnerships with high schools by offering dual credit courses for high school and college credit while also reaching forward to their four-year partners to provide a seamless transfer, and not just for students in traditional liberal arts transfer programs. The baby boomers, who swelled the community college ranks in the 1960s and 1970s, are back as they near or reach retirement; Hispanic student attendance is on the rise; and many colleges are becoming active in drawing international students, continuing to ensure a diverse community of learners.

THE FUTURE

Community colleges have struggled throughout their history to solidify their legitimacy as institutions of higher education. One one hand, community colleges were tightly coupled with high schools for many of their early years, and there are still many factors that confound the community college identity as an institution of higher learning. One factor is the role of community colleges in offering course work that is essentially high school level as they attempt to provide remediation to underprepared students. In addition, the faculty focus is on teaching as opposed to research; classes remain small and more similar to those in a high school setting than a university environment; colleges offer dual credit classes to high school students; and many community colleges do not currently offer the standard marker of achievement in higher education, the baccalaureate degree.

On the other hand, community colleges are also tightly coupled with four-year institutions through articulation agreements, reverse transfer, increased interest in the transfer of associate of applied science degrees, and the national goal to produce more college graduates. Brint and Karabel (1989) suggested over 20 years ago that it is not a problem for community colleges to connect the educational system with the world of work, and in 2010 this was the issue that drew the Obama administration's attention to these institutions. However, Brint and Karabel cautioned that "without strong and accessible transfer programs, the community college will have effectively abandoned its historic dream of bringing higher education to the people" (p. 230). The fact that community colleges have maintained their liberal arts transfer function continues to give legitimacy to their ties to higher education.

CONCLUSION

Although community colleges evolved from an elitist agenda, it did not take them long to become the egalitarian institutions of today. Over time, community colleges have evolved from institutions focused solely on providing the first two years of a baccalaureate education to institutions that offer career programs, developmental education, continuing education, adult education, high school equivalency preparation, English-as-a-second-language programs, workforce development, and more. Community colleges have built and expanded campuses, offered classes at all hours of the day and night, provided online options, and responded to the diverse needs of their diverse communities. They welcome everyone and try to serve everyone. Whether community colleges can continue to be everything to everyone while remaining responsive to the educational institutions below them and above them, as well as the communities around them, remains to be seen, but given their history in the past 110 years, there is reason to be optimistic.

REFERENCES

American Association of Community Colleges. (2013). *2013 community college fast facts*. Retrieved from http://www.aacc.nche.edu/AboutCC/Documents/ FactSheet2013.pdf

Badolato, V. (2010). *The future of higher education may depend on the success of community colleges*. Retrieved from http://www.ncsl.org/default.aspx?tabid=19380

Beach, J. M. (2011). *Gateway to opportunity? A history of the community college in the United States*. Sterling, VA: Stylus.

Brint, S., & Karabel, J. (1989). *The diverted dream: Community colleges and the promise of educational opportunity in America, 1900–1985*. New York, NY: Oxford University Press.

Carl D. Perkins Vocational Education Act of 1984, Pub. L. No. 98-524 (1984).

Carnegie Commission on Higher Education. (1970). *The open-door colleges: Policies for community colleges*. New York, NY: McGraw-Hill.

Cohen, A. M. (1998). *The shaping of American higher education: Emergence and growth of the contemporary system*. San Francisco, CA: Jossey-Bass.

Cohen, A. M. (2001). Governmental policies affecting community colleges: A historical perspective. In B. K. Townsend & S. B. Twombly (Eds.), *Community colleges: Policy in the future context* (pp. 3–22). Westport, CT: Ablex.

Drury, R. L. (2003). Community colleges in America: A historical perspective. *Inquiry*, *8*(1). Retrieved from http://www.vccaedu.org/inquiry/inquiry-spring2003/i-81-drury.html

Fike, D. S., & Fike, R. (2008). Predictors of first-year student retention in the community college. *Community College Review*, *36*(2), 68–88.

Hispanic Association of Colleges and Universities. (2013). *HACU: The champions of Hispanic success in higher education*. Retrieved from http://www.hacu.net/hacu/ default.asp

Illinois Board of Higher Education. (1998). *Illinois Articulation Initiative: Illinois transferable general education core curriculum*. Retrieved from http://www .transfer.org/IAI/FACT/Forms/IAILibrary/GEPanelDocument_1998-May-01 .pdf

Kasper, H. T. (2002–2003, Winter). The changing role of the community college. *Occupational Outlook Quarterly*. Retrieved from http://www.bls.gov/opub/ ooq/2002/winter/art02.pdf

Lach, I. (1998). *ICCS history*. Retrieved from http://www.iccb.state.il.us/history.html

Manpower Development and Training Act, Pub. L. No. 87-415, 76 Stat. 23 (1962). Retrieved from http://www.gpo.gov/fdsys/pkg/STATUTE-76/pdf/STATUTE-76-Pg23-2.pdf

National Defense Education Act, H.R. 13247, 85th Congress, Pub. L. No. 85-864 (1958).

Pascarella, E., & Terenzini, P. (2005). *How college affects students: Vol. 2, A third decade of research*. San Francisco, CA: Jossey-Bass.

Ratcliff, J. L. (n.d.). *Community colleges—the history of community colleges, the junior college and the research university: The community college mission*. Retrieved from http://education.stateuniversity.com/pages/1873/Community-Colleges.html

Rohder, K. (2010, Fall). Leading by example: How JJC's first president helped shape the future of community colleges in Illinois. *Joliet Junior College Connections*. Retrieved from http://www.jjc.edu/about/alumni/Documents/Fall%20Magz%202010.pdf

Rosenbaum, J. E., Deil-Amen, R., & Person, A. E. (2006). *After admission: From college access to college success*. New York, NY: Russell Sage Foundation.

Sterling, R. E. (2001). *Joliet Junior College 1901 to 2001: A pictorial history of America's oldest public community college*. St. Louis, MO: G. Bradley.

Vaughan, G. B. (2000). *The community college story* (2nd ed.). Washington, DC: Community College Press.

Vocational Education Act, Pub. L. No. 88-210 (1963).

The Wisconsin idea: History of the Wisconsin idea. (2013). Retrieved from http://wisconsinidea.wisc.edu/history-of-the-wisconsin-idea/

Witt, A. A., Wattenbarger, J. L., Gollattscheck, J. F., & Suppiger, J. E. (1994). *America's community colleges: The first century*. Washington, DC: Community College Press.

Wood, S. H. (1987). *The people's legacy: A history of Joliet Junior College 1901–1984* (2nd ed.). Joliet, IL: Joliet Junior College Foundation.

2

Community College Economic Climate, Policy Landscape, and the American Graduation Initiative

John L. Jamrogowicz

CHARLES DICKENS OPENED *A Tale of Two Cities* with "It was the best of times, it was the worst of times" (Lombardi, 2014, para. 2). As the ACPA–College Student Educators International Commission for Two-Year Colleges celebrated the 50th anniversary of its founding, the environment in which the American two-year college found itself could be similarly described. The Great Recession has contributed to record enrollment growth (Borden, 2010). The recession itself is showing signs of abatement and according to some experts is officially over (Lee, 2010). We are now in what has been referred to as a different, prolonged recovery. President Barack Obama showcased the community college as integral not only to sustained recovery from the recession but also to future American competitiveness in the world economy ("Remarks by the President on the American Graduation Initiative" [AGI], 2009 [hereafter cited as "Remarks by the President"]). In contrast, states across the country are almost uniformly enacting or contemplating reductions in spending on higher education, including community colleges (Katsinas & Friedel, 2010).

The ability to charge (and raise) tuition, a capability often cited by legislators or executives as mitigation for reductions in allocations, is monitored closely, and in at least some cases, even capped by those same legislators. An

17

additional consideration is that there are, and will continue to be, market limitations on how high tuition can go in relation to the number of people who will be able to afford college. This chapter endeavors to situate the current economic climate for community colleges in fostering a completion agenda as called for by the Obama administration's AGI ("Remarks by the President," 2009). However, to understand the positioning of the two-year sector and the importance of community colleges in postsecondary education, it is critical to reflect on the origination and expansion of these institutions.

ACCESS AND THE EXPANSION OF THE COMMUNITY COLLEGE MODEL

Cohen and Brawer (2008) asserted that, at least through the 1970s, the historical mission of the public two-year college can be summed up in one word—access. Whether because of insufficient academic preparation, long-term absence from an academic environment, insufficient financial resources to afford the costs associated with a four-year postsecondary education, or having been raised in an environment that did not provide encouragement or support to attain a postsecondary education, students with these characteristics have found that community colleges have had an open-door admissions policy focused on enabling college attendance rather than discouraging or denying that opportunity. After initially playing a predominantly general education or transfer role, since the 1970s community colleges have matured and developed technical education degree programs, diplomas, and certificates. Cohen and Brawer noted that the growth in the technical education area was also a result of previously separate technical education centers and vocational training colleges merging with or morphing into the community college. Today academic and business partnerships straddle what once was a line of clear distinction between the credit and the noncredit (continuing education) components of community colleges.

Although it has not been necessarily out of the ordinary for junior and, later, community colleges to evolve into four-year institutions, a somewhat recent phenomenon has been the introduction of the junior and senior years and the baccalaureate degree to two-year colleges (Walker, 2005). In most cases, these appear to have been market driven to counter the increasing costs of earning the baccalaureate at a four-year institution. On the surface at least, this development relates certainly to the access mission of the two-year college. However, it may also be argued that this represents not only a significant expansion in the scope of that mission but perhaps a complete redefinition of it. Townsend (2005) offered an excellent, concise exploration of those different perspectives, concluding that an applied baccalaureate may enable more students to attain that credential, but it will also generate discussion about the very definition of the baccalaureate itself. Moreover, it is too early to tell what its evolution may mean for the two-year college as an institutional type.

THE COMPLETION AGENDA AND THE
OBAMA ADMINISTRATION

The AGI, announced by President Obama in 2009, showcased community colleges as potential engines to drive the recovery from the Great Recession and a return of American dominance by increasing the proportion of the population with a college education. Projected growth for jobs requiring an associate's degree or better is expected to be twice that for jobs requiring no college ("Remarks by the President," 2009). Twelve billion dollars would have been provided if the initiative had been fully funded ("Remarks by the President," 2009), and even in an age of entire-industry bailouts costing hundreds of billions of dollars, that amount would have represented an appreciable investment in postsecondary education. The potential support from the federal government and the tuition hikes at four-year colleges that are outstripping increases in Pell Grants and other aid indicate that community colleges are perhaps poised to enjoy a best of times period.

However, by 2010 the original legislation associated with Obama's 2009 call to action—the Trade Adjustment Assistance Community College and Career Training Grants Program (U.S. Department of Labor, 2012)—provided $2 billion rather than the subsequent $12 billion for competitive grants spread over a four-year period (U.S. Department of Labor, 2013). It also included some funding for continued support of already existing job-training programs associated with two-year schools (Berube, 2010).

In 2013 there were 1,132 community colleges in the United States (American Association of Community Colleges [AACC], 2013). For example, the even distribution of the $2 billion among these colleges would result in about $1.8 million to each institution, which is a lot of money. However, spread over a number of years, it is not the kind of funding that would enable an institution to transform itself into anything beyond what it might already be. It is not very likely to enable administrators and faculty members at community colleges to respond to President Obama's call to action ("Remarks by the President," 2009) and spark a transformation in American postsecondary education and economic competitiveness. A missed opportunity qualifies for at least an honorable mention in a worst-of-times assessment.

A second dilemma confronting the federal government involves the overall economic and political environment, including a combination of the Great Recession of 2007–2009 with the ongoing deficit spending and associated problems that have been characteristics of the federal budget for years. This was best illustrated in President Obama's 2011 State of the Union address in which he called for sustained and increased investment in education, on the one hand, but proposed an across-the-board freeze in domestic program spending on the other. Those two positions seem to be mutually exclusive; however, both received applause from the congressional audience. In fact, his proposed fiscal year 2012 budget did call for a 4.3% increase in the allocation for the U.S. Department of Education (Lederman, 2011).

THE ROLE OF STATES IN ADDRESSING COMMUNITY COLLEGE FUNDING CHALLENGES

In the state arena, community colleges receive funding through a number of mechanisms and processes. Head count, amount and types of county or city funding, full-time student equivalent counts, library requirements, special equipment needs, costs associated with special programs or offerings, performance or accountability standards, previous funding levels, and geographic or demographic considerations are assessed in a variety of ways as part of the funding model (Mullin & Honeyman, 2007). Regardless of how states fund community colleges, their overall contributions have fallen to the point where only about one fifth of state higher education appropriations go to community colleges, resulting in an increasing reliance on tuition (Kelderman, 2011). The full-time student equivalency has a particularly troubling impact on community colleges when not offset by other funding considerations since community colleges typically have a higher proportion of part-time students compared to four-year institutions. That is, a six-credit-hour student makes the same demands on a college's financial aid, admissions, registrar, orientation, testing, counseling, and career development services as a 15-credit-hour student. Similarly, two part-time students take up two seats in a laboratory versus one seat occupied by one full-time student. This places more pressure on tuition as a source of funding, especially in times of higher than usual enrollment, to compensate for that difference and to hire faculty and staff.

Regarding physical and human resources, many community colleges have faced demand exceeding available physical space, seats, and instructional personnel (Katsinas & Friedel, 2010). Online courses have been popular and are becoming increasingly more so. Younger, more technologically savvy students may even be expecting online offerings. In fact, drawing from Larry D. Rosen, author of *Rewired: Understanding the iGeneration and How They Learn*, and Pamela K. Quinn, provost of the LeCroy Center for Educational Telecommunications for the Dallas County Community College District, Paul Bradley (2010a) described technology as being so enmeshed in the lives and psyches of today's 18- to 24-year-olds that a failure to meet their expectations may be seen essentially as tantamount to ignoring an integral element of their beings. Today's students not only prefer technology but also regard it as a part of their understanding of reality (Bradley, 2010a). At the same time, Bradley cited Jean M. Runyon, dean of the Virtual Campus at Anne Arundel Community College, who cautioned that even this tech-savvy population of students includes those who because of lack of access to the Internet, lack of experience with specific online tools, or personal learning style preferences may still require or respond better to more traditional forms of instruction. Thus, increased reliance on distance learning as a solution for meeting space demands may not be a definitive response (Bradley, 2010a).

In the student services arena, in-person services and learning are essential for some students because of any number of factors, including academic preparedness, self-discipline, maturity, learning style preferences, lack of technology skills outside social media and gaming, and lack of access to technology for students from lower socioeconomic environments. In any case, the relief that distance learning brings to physical space demands still has costs associated with keeping faculty and technology (hardware and software) current.

States often do not fund community colleges at full need, no matter how they calculate or determine need. In fact, taken together, direct state funding as a percentage of a community college's total operating expenses has been declining for years (Katsinas & Friedel, 2010; Kelderman, 2011). The decline is significant, as reflected by the designation *state assisted* rather than *state supported.* The $43 billion in federal economic stimulus funds provided through the American Recovery and Reinvestment Act of 2009 helped states provide about 35% of community college budgets versus the prerecession 25% funding level (Freking, 2010).

In a survey of members of the National Council of State Directors of Community Colleges, only 11 of the states reported specific planning for the end of the stimulus funding (Katsinas & Friedel, 2010), suggesting that the overall budget contribution would drop back to the 25% level. Continuing budget deficits are finding legislators less than eager to embrace increased higher education funding (Whoriskey, 2010). Thirty-eight states ranked Medicaid and the end of American Recovery and Reinvestment Act funding in second place (the recession itself was number one) as key drivers of state budgets in fiscal year 2009–2010 (Katsinas & Friedel, 2010). In addition, some reports suggested that an informal working group in the U.S. Congress was exploring the pros and cons of proposing legislation that would allow states to declare bankruptcy (Bullock, 2011). The effect on state-funded pensions, state-backed bonds, and state economies is difficult to forecast, as would be the net cumulative effect on community college support and enrollments. Local funding of community colleges also comes under increased pressures during a recession as cities and counties redirect funds because of losses of state and federal allocations.

Another funding-related issue with potentially profound implications for federal and state arenas is evolving. Although public community college student loans have not risen to the levels they have in the other sectors (public four-year, private four-year, and private two-year colleges), they are at a historical level. Some analysts fear a collapse of the financial aid loan market that could qualify as the next economic bubble to burst (Cronin & Horton, 2009). Just having to contemplate the prospect of that development may qualify for a worst-of-times designation. Currently, enrollment in two-year colleges is reaching full-capacity levels (Bradley, 2010b). Increases in Pell Grant funding and increased tuition revenue have helped offset some, but certainly not all, of the disruption in state, local, and other federal funding.

For the near future, many new jobs will require less than four years' education or training but more than a high school diploma or high school equivalency degree. Even if the enrollment peaks associated with the Great Recession begin to level off, the pace of change is such that increasing numbers of the currently employed are likely to return to community colleges for retraining. In fact, in a posting for *Forbes* that questions whether we are ready to deal with the pace of technological change, Hendrickson (2013) addresses the implications of estimates for the production of technical knowledge to double every one to two years and that today's average young person will experience at least 10 or more career changes. If these projections are accurate, the opportunity for community colleges to continue to play significant roles in American educational and workforce development life will be substantial.

However, increased enrollments in community colleges are of concern not only because of limited physical capacities. There are at least three additional ramifications. First, in some cases students who are headed toward program completion experience unanticipated delays as required courses become full. Especially in curricula with cyclical scheduling (perhaps a particular course is only offered in one term out of every academic year), this interruption can make the difference between persistence and dropping out or stopping altogether. Second, limited spaces present a challenge to the core access role community colleges play. For a student to have reached the point of registration only to face difficulties in finding classes frustrates the student and the institution (Ashburn, 2011; Lewin, 2010; Moltz, 2011). Third, according to Beach (2011), overcrowding in four-year institutions has caused more affluent middle- and upper-income students to enroll in community colleges. These students, who could otherwise afford the higher costs of four-year institutions and who tend to be better prepared academically, take advantage of the two-year open door and later transfer to complete a baccalaureate; this provides an additional disadvantage to students whose academic preparedness or socioeconomic standing makes them even more dependent on the open-access mission of community colleges.

THE PARADOX OF COLLEGE COMPLETION IN TWO-YEAR INSTITUTIONS

Community colleges have never been known for high graduation rates (Greenblatt, 2010). On the cusp of the great expansion that was about to take place in two-year education, Burton Clark (1960) applied Goffman's sociological concept of a "cooling-out" function to two-year colleges. He postulated that two-year colleges were society's way of softening the fact that not everyone was destined to attend and succeed in four-year colleges. In essence, higher education progression reflected a reality where brighter students accomplished bigger things and went on to more enhanced lives. Nonetheless, the community colleges did provide an avenue for some to enter four-year colleges or to attain an educational credential sufficient for at least entry into fields of work. Believers in the cooling-out theory would say that was a nice side effect but not the primary purpose of the community college education. This debate, in one form or another, persists to this day.

Low graduation rates are often a starting point for a discussion that ends with making the case that most unsuccessful community college students were probably never truly college material.

Two-year institutions respond typically along several lines of reasoning. With access as a primary mission and open-door admissions as a tool, it should be no wonder that graduation rates might not be a reasonable measure to judge community college effectiveness. Some two-year college students enroll with no intention of graduating, and an associate's degree is not necessary for transfer to a four-year institution. Some students pick particular courses to support employment promotional goals or may select a certificate or other nondegree option, which often are not counted in government graduation reports. Other students complete course work solely for self-improvement. Further, although the percentage of part-time students at some four-year colleges is increasing, community colleges have always seen higher proportions of part-time enrollment. These students have competing priorities in their lives, such as work and family, and graduating under those circumstances can be challenging. Part-time students also have difficulty in meeting government reporting standards such as graduation within three years. To account for these various factors, some contend that goal completion rates would be a fairer measure of the effectiveness of community colleges. However, capturing goal attainment rates (or other data for that matter) is further complicated by the "stopping-out" attendance pattern often associated with part-time and even full-time community college students. That is, an absence of a semester or two in enrollment does not signal necessarily that the student has dropped out or that a specific goal was attained or abandoned. It may merely reflect the economic, motivational, or personal circumstances associated with that student's attendance of college. These are a few of many issues associated with assessment and accountability in the community college arena. Cohen and Brawer (2008) provide a more comprehensive discussion of accountability.

If two-year colleges are to be the centerpieces of American job preparedness, then it will be necessary and expected that they produce the desired results. The AGI directs a doubling of the graduation rates within 10 years. A shift in emphasis from access to graduation assumes that policy, an institution, or society as a whole can do something about a graduation problem that has persisted since Clark (1960) took two-year colleges to task more than a half century ago. Furthermore, there seems to be an assumption that at least part of the answer involves an infusion of cash.

Consider two examples. Joseph Sample takes advantage of an innovative program at Exceptional Community College. The program involves a quick remediation course that uses an accelerated curriculum with a mixed mode of overlapping course work. In essence, Joseph can be working on one or more program requirements continuously via traditional classrooms, online components, and traditional and virtual laboratory experiences. To a great degree, Joseph controls how long it will take him to complete his program of study, earn his certificate or degree, and enter the job market newly trained, educated, and credentialed. However, just short of his capstone semester, Joseph hears of a job and applies for it. The application process involves an opportunity to demonstrate skill attainment and proficiencies. He passes with flying colors, is one of five people offered positions, and accepts the offer. Joseph does not complete his program of study. That fact may or may not become a problem for him. Had he chosen to complete his program, he may or may not have found the kind of employment he sought. It is difficult to argue that the administrators and faculty members at Exceptional have failed their funding agency, the local business, or Joseph.

In a second example, Joseph's daughter, Maria, is also enrolled at Exceptional Community College as a first-time, full-time freshman. She would prefer to be attending her state's flagship public university. However, her ACT and SAT scores were not competitive. University staff suggested that she complete 30 credit hours of study at Exceptional, including some remediation in mathematics. If she completes her Exceptional course work with a 2.5 grade point average or higher, the university will accept her and all but the remedial courses in transfer. Maria meets that standard, the university accepts her, and she enrolls. It is doubtful that either Maria or the university will find fault with her education at Exceptional.

Another issue underlying, and perhaps undermining, the debate about community college graduation and goal completion rates involves the gaps between the skill sets in reading, writing, mathematics, and analytical reasoning and problem-solving abilities developed in high school and those needed to be successful in college (Frey, 2010). The open doors of community colleges welcome students with such gaps. Increased focus on graduation, goal completion, or success rates could result in community colleges becoming less eager to open their doors to students like Joseph and Maria. Regardless of any other variables, students with lower skill levels find themselves placed almost immediately in a higher risk category relative to their chances of persisting and being successful in college. That is, they immediately require remediation (Borromeo, 2005). Not only does this have academic implications, but for many first-generation students (again, a more salient issue for community colleges than for four-year institutions) this perceived and actual step backward runs psychologically counter to what one would hope for any student. Depending on the scope of a particular student's remediation needs and his or her choice of academic program, anywhere from 3 to as many as 27 or more semester credit hours may be added to the student's program of study. This can add two or more full-time semesters. With some two-year degrees now requiring 70 or more semester credit hours, the total credit hour requirements for a two-year degree can approach or even exceed 100. This may test the limits of the Pell Grant and direct-lending lifetime maximum amounts, especially for students targeting an eventual baccalaureate.

Hauptmann (2011) offered a compelling discussion of the trend to focus on graduation or completion rates from colleges and offered some answers to questions posed earlier in this chapter. He contended that these graduation rates are one part of a more elaborate and more important "attainment rate pipeline," which looks ultimately at the "percentage of the working population who earn a degree" (Hauptmann, 2011, p. 3). Fixating on the graduation rate itself may cause one to overlook the fact that two of the ways to improve graduation rates are not necessarily healthy from an educational or economic perspective. Improved graduation rates could be achieved through lower standards or higher selectivity. Neither is acceptable in terms of eventually improving the attainment rate. Only by including a focus on quality as well as on the number of graduates will an improved graduation rate be meaningful.

Hauptmann (2011) contended that community colleges contribute greatly to our nation's relatively high participation rate in higher education. However, their contributions to graduation and attainment rates are less impressive. Regardless of the reasons for this, much of community colleges' contributions in the future will depend on the number of jobs and kinds of labor demands that will be present in the economy. The kinds of jobs may determine to what extent associate's degrees and certificates will evolve into being functional terminal credentials. In this regard, outlooks are probably good for community colleges. However, Hauptmann asserted that the future is uncertain; there could be a shortage of college graduates in relationship to job numbers or there could be fewer jobs because of a surplus of graduates. The former presents a greater challenge for the United States' worldwide economic competitiveness. But because a distinguishing characteristic of our nation's recovery from the Great Recession of 2007–2009 has been, at least through 2012 and into 2013, a relatively smaller literal growth in new jobs, then it could be that Hauptmann's latter scenario would be accentuated and present an even greater challenge to the United States' economy.

SIGN OF THE TIMES

In the current vernacular, it is what it is. Administrators and faculty members of public community colleges face a coalescence of an economic downturn, budget crises (federal, state, and local) and associated budget cuts, renewed demands for graduation rates to be used as accountability standards, and continuing expectations of maintaining the open door of access to post-secondary education. Tuition increases will continue to be both an answer and a problem. Reductions in state and federal assistance will exert force for increases, but politicians and consumers may balk at increases.

If graduation rates are established as the measure of accountability, community colleges, especially in the face of budget crises, will be challenged to resist reducing access or lowering curriculum standards as a means of meeting that measure. Whether certificate credentials make their way into graduation and attainment rate calculations will likely depend on whether they solidify themselves as ways to gain, maintain, or improve one's employment status.

Despite improvements that may or may not evolve in K–12 education, community college administrators and faculty members will still face the challenge of not only providing the learning environment expected of college-level work but also remediating students who are underprepared and adult students returning to school rusty in the basics after years of being away from formal educational settings. Although the marketplace and accountability factors may compel community colleges to focus more intently on the shorter certificate credential, continued cost and capacity issues at four-year colleges will likely mean a continued growth in community colleges' transfer function.

Even though we cannot predict the future, one can assume that the community college will look remarkably different before we reach the 100th anniversary of ACPA's Commission for Two-Year Colleges. To a large extent, whether community colleges become front and center in American higher education's interface with the world of work and economic development will depend on the extent to which we meet these challenges. Doing so may require transformative changes in terms of how we measure a community college's success. How well and, perhaps, how quickly we make these changes may determine whether we look back and view these as the best of times or the worst of times for community colleges.

REFERENCES

American Association of Community Colleges. (2013). *2013 community college fast facts*. Retrieved from http://www.aacc.nche.edu/AboutCC/Documents/FactSheet 2013.pdf

Ashburn, E. (2011, February 9). Community-college students say they struggle to get into needed classes. *The Chronicle of Higher Education*. Retrieved from http://chronicle.com/article/Community-College-Students-Say/126303/

Beach, J. M. (2011). *Gateway to opportunity? A history of the community college in the United States*. Sterling, VA: Stylus.

Berube, A. (2010, March 23). The end of the American graduation initiative [Web log post]. Retrieved from http://www.brookings.edu/blogs/the-avenue/posts/2010/03/23-agi-berube

Borden, V. M. (2010). Down means up: Community college enrollment surges as economy sags. *Community College Week*, *23*(8), 7, 10–11. Retrieved from http://www.ccweek.com/news/articlefiles/2198-CCW112910-AllPages3.pdf

Borromeo, D. (2005, September 12). *State policies undermine public school reform*. Retrieved from http://www.highereducation.org/news/news_090805.shtml

Bradley, P. (2010a, May 17). Future shock. *Community College Week*, *22*(20), 6–8.

Bradley, P. (2010b, November 29). Shifting emphasis: Completion agenda dominates even as colleges struggle with enrollment climb. *Community College Week*, *23*(8), 6–9.

Bullock, N. (2011, February 15). Lawmakers resist bankruptcy for US states. *Financial Times*. Retrieved from http://www.cnbc.com/id/41595577

Clark, B. R. (1960). The "cooling out" function in higher education. *The American Journal of Sociology*, *65*(6), 569–576.

Cohen, A. M., & Brawer, F. B. (2008). *The American community college* (5th ed.). San Francisco, CA: Jossey-Bass.

Cronin, J. M., & Horton, H. E. (2009, May 22). Will higher education be the next bubble to burst? *The Chronicle of Higher Education*. Retrieved from http://chronicle.com/article/Will-Higher-Education-Be-the/44400

Freking, K. (2010, December 1). *Report: States face more financial stress. U-T San Diego*. Retrieved from http://www.signonsandiego.com/news/2010/dec/01/report-states-face-more-financial-stress/

Frey, C. (2010, August 16). A crash course in college preparedness. *U.S. News & World Report*. Retrieved from http://www.usnews.com/education/articles/2010/08/16/a-crash-course-in-college-preparedness

Greenblatt, A. (2010). *For community colleges: A hard lesson in politics*. Retrieved from http://www.npr.org/templates/story/story.php?storyId=125225059

Hauptmann, A. M. (2011). *Increasing higher education attainment in the United States: Challenges and opportunities*. Retrieved from http://www.aei.org/files/2011/02/15/Increasing%20Higher%20Education%20Attainment%20in%20the%20United%20States%20-%20Challenges%20and%20Opportunities%20by%20Arthur%20Hauptman.pdf

Hendrickson, M. (2013). *Technology may spur 10+ career changes for today's youth: Are we ready?* Retrieved from http://www.forbes.com/sites/markhendrickson/2013/07/04/technology-may-spur-10-career-changes-for-todays-youth-are-we-ready/

Katsinas, S. G., & Friedel, J. N. (2010). *Uncertain recovery: Access and funding issues in public higher education*. Retrieved from http://www.cscconline.org/index.php/download_file/view/85/247/

Kelderman, E. (2011, February 6). As state funds dry up, many community colleges rely more on tuition than on taxes to get by. *The Chronicle of Higher Education*. Retrieved from http://chronicle.com/article/As-State-Funds-Dry-Up/126240/

Lederman, D. (2011, February 15). Maximum Pell, at all costs. *Inside Higher Ed*. Retrieved from http://www.insidehighered.com/news/2011/02/15/obama_budget_would_sustain_5_550_pell_cut_subsidy_for_graduate_students

Lee, D. (2010, September 21). Recession's over, economists say to a skeptical public. *Los Angeles Times*. Retrieved from http://articles.latimes.com/2010/sep/21/business/la-fi-recession-over-20100921

Lewin, T. (2010, June 23). Community colleges cutting back on open access. *New York Times*. Retrieved from http://www.nytimes.com/2010/06/24/education/24community.html

Lombardi, E. (2014). *A tale of two cities quotes*. Retrieved from http://classiclit.about.com/od/taleoftwocities/a/aa_tale_2citqu.htm

Moltz, D. (2011, February 9). Left in the hall. *Inside Higher Ed*. Retrieved from http://www.insidehighered.com/news/2011/02/09/community_college_students_had_trouble_enrolling_in_fall_2010

Mullin, C. M., & Honeyman, D. S. (2007). The funding of community colleges: A typology of state funding formulas. *Community College Review, 35*(2), 113–127. Retrieved from http://crw.sagepub.com/content/35/2/113.full.pdf

Obama, B. (2011, January 25). *State of the Union address*. Retrieved from http://www.huffingtonpost.com/2011/01/25/obama-state-of-the-union-_1_n_813478.html

Remarks by the president on the American Graduation Initiative. (2009). Retrieved from http://www.whitehouse.gov/the_press_office/Remarks-by-the-President-on-the-American-Graduation-Initiative-in-Warren-MI/

Townsend, B. K. (2005). A cautionary view. In D. L. Floyd, M. L. Skolnik, & K. P. Walker (Eds.), *The community college baccalaureate: Emerging trends and policy issues* (pp. 179–190). Sterling, VA: Stylus.

U.S. Department of Labor. (2012). *Trade Adjustment Assistance Community College and Career Training Grant Program: Laws and regulations.* Retrieved from http://www.doleta.gov/taaccct/lawregulations.cfm

U.S. Department of Labor. (2013). *Trade Adjustment Assistance Community College and Career Training Grant Program: Program summary.* Retrieved from http://www.doleta.gov/taaccct/

Walker, K. P. (2005). History, rationale, and the community college baccalaureate association. In D. L. Floyd, M. L. Skolnik, & K. P. Walker (Eds.), *The community college baccalaureate: Emerging trends and policy issues* (pp. 9–23). Sterling, VA: Stylus.

Whoriskey, P. (2010, November 27). Community colleges are getting an education in tough economics. *Washington Post.* Retrieved from http://www.washingtonpost.com/wp-dyn/content/story/2010/11/27/ST2010112700079.html

3

College Readiness and the Open-Door Mission

Patricia Munsch, Tania Velazquez, and Corinne Kowpak

I N 1946 PRESIDENT HARRY S. TRUMAN set the path for the policy of open access and the open-door mission of community colleges (Thelin, 2004). The goal of open access in higher education was to provide equality for all who sought to advance in their education while investing in the future of the United States. "An open door mission is a commitment to providing comprehensive programs and services for all of the constituents in their communities regardless of racial, ethnic, economic or academic circumstances" (Bragg, 2001, p. 96).

Because of the open-door mission and the subsequent development of curricula, programs, and services, "the community college is the single largest and most important portal into higher education" (Dougherty, 1998, p. 1). In fact, in *Keeping America's Promise: A Report on the Future of the Community College*, Boswell and Wilson (2004) stated, "Perhaps one of the most fundamental developments at the end of the 20th century is that opportunity in this country is more and more a function of education, and that reality is something that sets America apart" (p. 7).

The following enrollment statistics demonstrate that many more who are seeking education have turned to open-access institutions:

> In October 2007, some 3.1 million young adults, or 11% of all 18- to 24-year-olds, were enrolled in a community college. A year later, that figure rose to 3.4

31

million students, or 12% of all 18- to 24-year-olds. By contrast, enrollments at four-year colleges were essentially flat from 2007 to 2008. (Fry, 2009, p. 1)

The open-door mission of community colleges greatly influences student affairs practice. The purpose of this chapter is to explore the concept of the open-door mission, discuss the challenges and opportunities associated with the policy of open access, and provide insight into the implications this policy has on the work of student affairs.

CHALLENGES AND OPPORTUNITIES

Despite the accolades that open access receives, there are challenges to supporting a diverse student population. Cohen and Brawer (2008) pointed out that community college faculty and staff are charged with serving a growing number of underprepared students with minimal resources along with working to serve all other populations of students on campus. Critics have argued that using community colleges as a form of equity within the educational structure is negligent because these institutions tend to be commuter-based campuses with inefficient funding and limited educational opportunities (Richardson & Bender, 1987). In spite of funding limitations, community college leaders view the open-access mission as a challenge and opportunity. The challenge lies in the allocation of limited resources to create opportunities for the students who come to community college with their wide range of needs. Of particular interest are the challenges and opportunities presented by a mission of open access on remedial education, often referred to as developmental education; at-risk students; and persistence.

Developmental Education

Enrollment growth created by the open-access mission embraced since the 1960s created new responsibilities for educators to assist underprepared students. Individuals entered college despite a lack of college preparation (Dotzler, 2003). As a result, community college administrators instituted developmental education programs that generally consisted of mathematics, English, and reading courses (Perin, 2005). By 1994 an estimated 650,000 students, or about one third of the freshmen entering college in the United States, were required to enroll in at least one developmental education course (Boylan, Bonham, & Bliss, 1994). Current research reports that 60% of students entering community colleges need at least one remedial course (Bailey, 2009; Bailey, Jeong, & Cho, 2010; Levin & Calcagno, 2008).

There is no consistency in state requirements or mandates about offering developmental education programs (Perin, 2005), a discrepancy that led to a scrutiny of remedial educational methods. Negative aspects of developmental education programs include the lack of credit given for remedial education, extended time that students must attend college, and the limited number of credits completed by students enrolled in such programs (Perin, 2005).

Assessment of the outcomes of developmental education has found mixed results. A series of research studies suggested that upon completion of their developmental education course work, students were able to complete subsequent academic course work, persist through college, and graduate (Bettinger & Long, 2005, 2009; Boylan & Bonham, 1994; Haeuser, 1993; Seybert & Soltz, 1992; Wallier, 1987). However, Matorell and McFarlin (2011) found that remediation had little effect on academic persistence or future educational pursuits. Calcagno and Long (2009) conducted a comprehensive study of remedial education in Florida and found an increase in persistence, but the impact was minimal on degree completion. One of the conclusions drawn from the study was that the implementation of remedial education placements and the characteristics of the students also influence persistence and degree completion.

College administrators and faculty face challenges with the growing number of underprepared students. Understanding the motivation and persistence of underprepared students is central to understanding their success. Ray, Garavalia, and Murdock (2003) found that the strongest predictors of success of students enrolled in developmental courses were their own personal self-regulating strategies, such as organizing their work, setting goals, and working to meet assigned deadlines. The research also indicated that students with an intrinsic goal orientation and value for academic work were motivated to continue their education and, as a result, successfully completed their developmental course work.

A number of institutions established learning communities as a method of working with students in need of developmental education. Barbatis (2010) sought to understand factors that promote or hinder student retention and examined the effect of learning communities on community college students in developmental education programs. Four main themes emerged regarding attributes that contribute to student retention. The first theme identified pre-college attributes, such as goal orientation, resourcefulness, determination, cultural and racial identity, and faith, as important factors in student persistence.

The second theme discussed the sense of support from families, including parents, siblings, grandparents, cousins, and significant others. The third theme noted social involvement, for example, membership in campus organizations and interactions with other students. The fourth theme was academic integration, or the students' relationships with faculty, understanding of college expectations, and establishment of effective study habits (Barbatis, 2010).

At-Risk Factors

The open-access mission provides opportunities for students who are at risk of not succeeding in higher education. Bragg (2001) noted that community colleges enroll more students with at-risk characteristics than their four-year counterparts. The National Center for Education Statistics (NCES, 2011) found that more than 70% of students who first enroll in community colleges possess at least one factor and 50% possess two or more factors that are known to place a student at risk of not succeeding in college. At-risk characteristics include the type of secondary school attainment (high school dropout) and stopping their education while the students are in college. According to Stratton, O'Toole, and Wetzel (2008), the definition of *stop out* is withdrawing by the start of a student's second year but returning within one year. Additional at-risk attributes include part-time enrollment and full-time employment while enrolled in college. Students who are financially independent, have dependents, or are single parents face challenges that also place them in the at-risk category (NCES, 2011). Other research on the field of higher education includes the following at-risk factors: first-generation college student, placement in developmental or remedial education courses, lower socioeconomic status, being a minority student, and having disabilities (Allen, Robbins, & Sawyer, 2009; Boylan, 2009; Perin, 2005).

One of the primary characteristics of at-risk students is lower academic preparedness (Adelman, 2005; Thayer, 2000). In some instances, students barely graduate from high school. In addition, high schools have been found to place fewer academic demands on students than in the past. Students may pass their classes but are challenged less by their teachers (Adelman, 2005). Unfortunately, they do not realize they are not prepared for the demands of a college classroom until they actually attend.

A second characteristic of students at risk is a lack of knowledge about the higher education system. They lack the knowledge of the bureaucratic operations of higher education (Thayer, 2000). This may be because they are first-generation students (those whose parents do not have a college degree). They may not have anyone who can educate them on college jargon to ensure their success at the college (Adelman, 2005; Thayer, 2000). Common challenges related to college knowledge include understanding the admission process, correctly filing for financial aid, understanding the registration process, and attending to each of these functions in a timely fashion.

Students at risk also have psychosocial characteristics that are different from those of typical students. These students encounter a cultural conflict between home and the college campus (Porchea, Allen, Robbins, & Phelps, 2010; Thayer, 2000). Many times the students may be the only ones from their homes enrolled in school. Their families and friends may not understand the pressure of schoolwork. They have more difficulty acclimating themselves to college once they are enrolled (Porchea et al., 2010), and there may be a conflict with cultural values or ethnic values as well (Miller & Murray, 2005; Porchea et al., 2010).

The socioeconomic characteristics of students at risk are also unique. Many of these students have low monetary resources. They have a lack of economic support from parents and therefore they often have to work to pay living expenses as well as their educational expenses. In many situations, the number of hours students work interferes with their dedication to school. As a result, they may have to enroll on a part-time basis. However, even though they may struggle with the social, academic, and economic adjustment to attending school, they do possess a strong desire to accomplish degree goals. The students express a high level of commitment to earning a degree. Based on their own economic struggles, this population of students is very motivated in their academic pursuits and believe that earning a degree will provide them with more economic resources (Porchea et al., 2010; Thayler, 2006).

Persistence

As a result of President Barack Obama's 2020 college completion goal, persistence to graduation has become a major issue in community colleges (Kanter, Ochoa, Nassif, & Chong, 2011). The president's strategic vision and goals include "10 million more graduates from community colleges, four-year colleges and universities by 2020" (Kanter et al., 2011, p. 10), which would increase the U.S. college degree attainment rate from 40% to 60%. Community colleges face a series of obstacles in working to achieving the presidential mandate. A series of studies indicate that students who begin their undergraduate education in a community college are less likely to reach their educational goals to earn a four-year college degree (Christie &

Hutcheson, 2003; Crook & Lavin, 1989; Dougherty, 1987, 1994; Pascarella & Terenzini, 2005; Rouse, 1995). Wang (2009) sought to understand why this phenomenon exists and identified a series of attributes that influence the success rates of transfer students, which include gender (female students are more likely to earn a four-year degree) and socioeconomic status (students from families with higher incomes are more likely to earn a four-year degree). In addition, students who originally enrolled in an academic curriculum versus a vocational curriculum had higher graduation rates. Consistent with other findings, student involvement in extracurricular activities was also a predictor in four-year degree completion. Finally, students' community college grade point average was an indicator of future success; those with higher cumulative grade point averages from community college were more likely to earn a baccalaureate degree. Lee, Mackie-Lewis, and Marks (1993) found similar results regarding persistence rates. The two strongest predictors of persistence and degree completion were cumulative grade point average and full-time study.

A major obstacle to degree completion is course offerings. Students can persist only if the college offers the courses necessary for degree completion. Lewin (2010) pointed out the overenrollment in community colleges has led to decreased opportunity for students to register and complete courses in a timely fashion. Lewin found that students were unable to register for the necessary courses because of the limited number of sections because of the growing student body. Today, many community colleges are enrolling students well past the capacity of the college in an effort to serve all students. As a result there are reduced funding per student, increased time to graduation, and frustrated students and faculties (Vaughan, 2003).

Although community colleges thrive on the open-access mission, it does present challenges in practice. Developmental education, students with at-risk attributes, and the pressure to increase persistence and degree completion all create obstacles unique to community colleges.

THE STUDENT AFFAIRS ROLE IN SUPPORTING OPEN ACCESS

Leaders in open-access institutions must recognize the varied needs of the diverse student populations served by their mission. There is a clear responsibility for community college faculty, staff, and administrators to provide additional support services to students who may be at risk for academic failure.

Considering the unique characteristics of students, faculty and staff can implement programs to help underprepared students become resilient and succeed academically. Successful student support programs have targeted academic advising and placements. Student assessments have gone beyond cognitive testing to include student readiness indicators and support measures. Support for students has increased through ongoing academic advising to provide a course of direction and support while the student is in a college program (Boylan, 2009). The organizational structure of such a program is also important; for example, developing partnerships with the student support program and other services on campus will increase the likelihood of student success (Levin, Cox, Cerven, & Haberler, 2010).

A commitment to the program from institutional leaders to ensure the success of the program is also necessary. Institutional leaders need to be committed to fully funding and staffing the program, and the faculty in the program need to be committed to serving at-risk students. Administrators can provide faculty teaching and learning training specially geared toward developmental course work (Levin et al., 2010).

Community college student affairs professionals who understand the population served by their institution can easily see how factors outside those related to students' educational pursuits can create insurmountable obstacles for many at-risk students. Anticipating student needs and striving to be proactive guides the work of those directly involved in supporting these students.

Research has found that student services, when structured in a committed, well-organized, and well-funded program, result in a significant increase in student success (Levin et al., 2010). The Community College Survey of Student Engagement (CCSSE, 2013) found that 59% of students reported using their academic advising services sometimes or often. Just over 70% indicated that their institutions place quite a bit or very much emphasis on providing support for students to succeed, 46% of students reported never or rarely using peer tutoring, and 42% reported using an academic skills lab (CCSSE, 2013). These data document that one size (or program) does not fit all. Students use services differently, and student services need to provide a broad scope of services in a variety of formats to best serve the diverse student population.

CONCLUSION

Providing services to support student success has been the motivating force behind student affairs work at community colleges. Helfgot (1998) noted that it "has been the organizing principle for community college student affairs work" (p. 30). He stated the reason quite simply: "Generally speaking, [community college students] have fewer advantages and more obstacles to overcome, so they need more help to succeed" (p. 30). Moreover, the motivation is clear: if community colleges are to continue as access points, then the revolving door of failure experienced by many students who enroll at community colleges must be avoided. The institution must commit to providing quality services to support student success (Helfgot, 2005).

This places a responsibility on student affairs professionals to renew their understanding of the student body, continually assess the services provided, and use data to make changes or enhancements to their offerings. Student affairs professionals who are cognizant of the missions of their institution and their division and remain in tune with the ever-changing needs of the community college student population can find their work challenging and rewarding. They are part of an organization that must be agile and responsive. "This is the way we have always done it" cannot be the justification for an approach to working with students. Instead, change must be viewed in a positive light. Responsive administrators will be at the cutting edge of our profession, taking the lead in forging new ways to provide services for students. Student affairs professionals in community colleges must always remain cognizant of the open-access mission, the goal of equality, and their role in promoting access and equity.

REFERENCES

Adelman, C. (2005). *Moving into town—and moving on: The community college in the lives of traditional-age students.* Washington, DC: U.S. Department of Education.

Allen, J., Robbins, S. B., & Sawyer, R. (2009). Can measuring psychosocial factors promote college success? *Applied Measurement in Education, 23*(1), 1–22. doi:10.1080/08957340903423503

Bailey, T. (2009). Challenge and opportunity: Rethinking the role and function of developmental education in community college. *New Directions for Community Colleges,* (145), 11–30.

Bailey, T., Jeong, D. W., & Cho, S. W. (2010). Referral, enrollment, and completion in developmental education sequences in community colleges. *Economics of Education Review, 29*(2), 255–270.

Barbatis, P. (2010). Underprepared, ethnically diverse community college students: Factors contributing to persistence. *Journal of Developmental Education, 33*(3), 14–28.

Bettinger, E., & Long, B. (2005). Remediation at the community college: Student participation and outcomes. *New Directions for Community Colleges*, (129), 17–26.

Bettinger, E., & Long, B. (2009). Addressing the needs of under-prepared college students: Does college remediation work? *Journal of Human Resources*, *44*, 736–771.

Boswell, K., & Wilson, C. D. (Eds.). (2004). *Keeping America's promise: A report on the future of the community college.* Retrieved from http://www.ecs.org/clearinghouse/53/09/5309.pdf

Boylan, H. R. (2009). Targeted intervention for developmental education students (T.I.D.E.S.). *Journal of Developmental Education*, *32*(3), 14–28.

Boylan, H. R., & Bonham, B. S. (1994). The impact of developmental education programs. *Review of Research in Developmental Education*, *9*(5), 120–132.

Boylan, H. R., Bonham, B. S., & Bliss, L. B. (1994). Who are the developmental students? *Research in Developmental Education*, *11*(2), 1–4.

Bragg, D. D. (2001). Community college access, mission and outcomes: Considering intriguing intersections and challenges. *Peabody Journal of Education*, *76*(1), 93–116.

Calcagno, J. C., & Long, B. T. (2009). *Evaluating the impact of remedial education in Florida community colleges: A quasi-experimental regression discontinuity design* (National Center for Postsecondary Research brief). New York, NY: Teachers College, Columbia University.

Christie, R., & Hutcheson, P. (2003). The net effects of "traditional" students. *Community College Review*, *31*(2), 1–20.

Cohen, A. M., & Brawer, F. B. (2008). *The American community college* (5th ed.). San Francisco, CA: Jossey-Bass.

Community College Survey of Student Engagement. (2013). *Key findings.* Retrieved from http://www.ccsse.org/survey/survey.cfm

Crook, D., & Lavin, D. (1989, May). *The community college effect revisited: The long-term impact of community college entry on BA attainment.* Paper presented at the meeting of the American Educational Research Association, San Francisco, CA.

Dotzler, J. J. (2003). A note on the nature and history of post-secondary development education in America. *Mathematics and Computer Education*, *37*(1), 121–126.

Dougherty, K. J. (1987). The effects of community colleges: Aid or hindrance to socioeconomic attainment? *Sociology of Education*, *60*(2), 86–103.

Dougherty, K. J. (1994). *The contradictory college: The conflicting origins, impacts, and futures of the community college.* Albany, NY: SUNY Press.

Dougherty, K. J. (1998). *Community college scenarios: Prospects and perils facing a mature and complex institution.* Unpublished manuscript, Community College Research Center, Teachers College, Columbia University, New York, NY.

Fry, R. (2009). *College enrollment hits all-time high, fueled by community college surge.* Retrieved from Pew Research Center website: http://pewresearch.org/pubs/1391/college-enrollment-all-time-high-community-college-surge

Haeuser, P. N. (1993). *Public accountability and developmental (remedial) education.* Retrieved from ERIC database. (ED356003)

Helfgot, S. R. (1998). The student success imperative. In M. M. Culp & S. R. Helfgot (Eds.), *Life at the edge of the wave: Lessons from the community college* (pp. 29–47). Washington, DC: NASPA–Student Affairs Administrators in Higher Education.

Helfgot, S. R. (2005). Core values and major issues in student affairs practice: What really matters? *New Directions for Community Colleges,* (131), 5–18.

Kanter, M., Ochoa, E., Nassif, R., & Chong, F. (2011, July). *Meeting President Obama's 2020 college completion goal.* Retrieved from http://www.ed.gov/sites/default/files/winning-the-future.ppt

Lee, V. E., Mackie-Lewis, C., & Marks, H. M. (1993). Persistence to the baccalaureate degree for students who transfer from community college. *American Journal of Education, 102*(2), 80–114.

Levin, H. M., & Calcagno, J. C. (2008). Remediation in the community college: An evaluator's perspective. *Community College Review, 35*(3), 181–207.

Levin, J. S., Cox, E. M., Cerven, C., & Haberler, Z. (2010). The recipe for promising practices in community colleges. *Community College Review, 38*(1), 31–43.

Lewin, T. (2010, June 24). Community colleges cutting back on open access. *New York Times,* pp. A15, A17.

Matorell, P., & McFarlin, L. (2011). Help or hindrance? The effects of college remediation on academic and labor market outcomes. *The Review of Economics and Statistics, 93*(2), 436–454.

Miller, M. A., & Murray, C. (2005). *Advising academically underprepared students.* Retrieved from http://www.nacada.ksu.edu/Clearinghouse/AdvisingIssues/Academically-Underprepared.htm

National Center for Education Statistics. (2011). *Trends in attainment among student populations at increased risk of no completion: Selected years, 1989–90 to 2008–09.* Retrieved from http://nces.ed.gov/pubs2012/2012254.pdf

Pascarella, E., & Terenzini, P. (2005). *How college affects students: Vol. 2, A third decade of research.* San Francisco, CA: Jossey-Bass.

Perin, D. (2005). Institutional decision making for increasing academic preparedness in community colleges. *New Directions for Community Colleges,* (129), 27–38.

Porchea, S. F., Allen, J., Robbins, S., & Phelps, R. P. (2010). Predictors of long-term enrollment and degree outcomes for community college students: Integrating academic, psychosocial, socio-demographic, and situational factors. *The Journal of Higher Education, 81,* 750–778.

Ray, M., Garavalia, L., & Murdock, T. (2003). Aptitude, motivation and self-regulation as predictors of achievement among developmental college students. *Research and Teaching in Developmental Education, 20*(1), 5–20.

Richardson, R. C., & Bender, L. W. (1987). *Fostering minority access and achievement in higher education.* San Francisco, CA: Jossey-Bass.

Rouse, C. (1995). Democratization or diversion? The effect of community colleges on educational attainment. *Journal of Business and Economic Statistics, 13*(2), 217–224.

Seybert, J. A., & Soltz, D. F. (1992). *Assessing the outcomes of developmental courses at Johnson County Community College.* Retrieved from ERIC database. (ED349052)

Stratton, L. S., O'Toole, D. M., &Wetzel, J. N. (2008). A multinomial logit model of college stopout and dropout behavior. *Economics of Education Review, 27*(3), 319–331.

Thayer, P. B. (2000). *Retention of students from first generation and low income backgrounds.* Retrieved from ERIC database. (ED446633)

Thelin, J. (2004). *A history of American higher education.* Baltimore, MD: Johns Hopkins University Press.

Vaughan, G. G. (2003, December 5). Redefining "open access." *The Chronicle of Higher Education,* p. B24.

Wallier, R. D. (1987, May). *A longitudinal study of guided studies students.* Retrieved from ERIC database. (ED293432)

Wang, X. (2009). Baccalaureate attainment and college persistence of community college transfer students at four-year institutions. *Research in Higher Education, 50,* 570–588. doi:10.1007/s11162-009-9133-z

4

Technology

The New Core Competency

Susan J. Procter and Julie Uranis

ECHNOLOGICAL LITERACY IS "as fundamental to a person's ability to navigate through society as traditional skills like reading, writing, and arithmetic" (U.S. Department of Education, 1996, p. 5). Computers are a staple in today's society and play a pivotal role in the economy. Yet despite the prevalence of technology and the mandates of No Child Left Behind (NCLB, 2002), students continue to arrive at postsecondary institutions with varied levels of technological literacy. Nowhere is this issue more relevant than in community colleges, where students from diverse backgrounds seek to obtain sub-baccalaureate credentials in technologically demanding professions.

DEFINING *TECHNOLOGICAL LITERACY*

Reviewing the literature, one can find any number of definitions for *technological literacy*; no standard definition exists. The plethora of terms used to refer to technological literacy in the literature clouds the concept even further. It is not uncommon to see terms such as *computer literacy*, *technology literacy*, and *computer proficiency* used interchangeably (Gaide, 2004; Trotter, 2009; Wilkinson, 2006).

According to a report by the Committee on Information Technology Literacy (National Research Council [NRC], 1999), being technologically literate means understanding computer terminology and computer use; actually using a computer is not required (van Vliet, Kletke, & Chakraborty, 1994). Much like technology, the definition of *technological literacy* has changed dramatically over the past several decades. Definitions vary widely, especially across research studies. For example, Nichols (2012) defined *computer literacy* as familiarity with computer components and the ability to use a computer to generate information. One of the most comprehensive definitions for *technological literacy* is in *Technically Speaking: Why All Americans Need to Know More About Technology* (Committee on Technological Literacy, National Research Council, 2002), where it is described as three interdependent dimensions: knowledge, ways of thinking and acting, and capabilities. This chapter focuses on the latter definition of *technological literacy* given its inclusion of knowledge and application of technology, both key components for student success at community colleges. The use of a specific definition allows for review of written policies that address technological literacy and consideration for how these measures can be integrated throughout the community college curriculum.

NEED FOR TECHNOLOGICAL LITERACY

The prominence of technological literacy as a national issue is evident in NCLB (2002). Although NCLB mandated that children be technologically literate by the eighth grade, NCLB left state governments to determine how to achieve this goal and evaluate their success. In granting license to each state government to determine these measures, the federal government essentially sanctioned the creation of multiple definitions of *technological literacy*.

Some students, mainly those in predominantly White and middle-class schools, have increased access to technology, but this is not the case for all students, as passage of NCLB did not change the reality of underserved populations and high-poverty schools (Goode, 2010a). A report by the National Education Technology Plan (U.S. Department of Education, 2010) described a critical national need for new educational strategies to address the lack of technological preparation students receive in P–12 schools. Until these strategies are successfully implemented, the responsibility for technological literacy falls to postsecondary institutions, in particular, community colleges (Wilkinson, 2006).

Passage of NCLB created expectations that students will arrive on college campuses with the technological skills needed to succeed (Trotter, 2009). Educational leaders assume that digital natives or the net generation, those raised with computers and the Internet, already possess the technological skills needed to succeed. However, this is an incorrect assumption. The digital divide persists, and as Goode (2010b) noted, it is indicative of the economic and social inequalities that exist in P–16 education. As Jones, Johnson-Yale, Millermaier, and Perez (2009) observed, nonminority students were more likely to be introduced to technology in their home environments, whereas Hispanic and Black non-Hispanic students were more likely to begin using Internet technologies at school. Privileged students, or those with access to technology in their school and home environments, can develop more skills and a greater diversity of skills simply because of the access they enjoy (Hargittai, 2010). The inequalities of access can have a profound and lasting impact on minority students, influencing their attitudes and decisions regarding future academic and career goals (Goode, 2010b).

Yet "access to information technology is not the same as proficiency in the use of information technology" (McManus, 2006, p. 44). According to Vaidhyanathan (2008), surfing the Internet and posting on Facebook do little to provide the technological competencies necessary to succeed in education. He further noted that generalizations of technological competency across an entire generation disregard the skills and experience of those who are not as socially or financially privileged. It is inconceivable to think that all students are "cyberkids" who possess high levels of competency with technology (Messineo & DeOllos, 2005, p. 51). The very need for NCLB (2002) legislation indicates otherwise.

The disparity in technological competencies has become increasingly obvious to postsecondary personnel as students adept at using technology for social networking and downloading music lack the basic skills required to complete course assignments (Vaidhyanathan, 2008). In particular, women, Hispanic and African American students, and students whose parents have less education tend to demonstrate less technological competence (Vaidhyanathan, 2008). These are the same demographic groups historically served by community colleges.

For community college students, technological literacy is a crucial component in the transition to a four-year institution and the workplace. Administrators and faculty at four-year institutions expect transfer students to have the technological skills to make a smooth transition to a new postsecondary environment (Cummings & Buzzard, 2002). Most colleges and universities require students to use technology for student business (e.g., registration, financial aid, scholarships) and to access course materials (Goode, 2010a). As community colleges and four-year institutions adopt distance education technology, technological literacy has become an implied prerequisite in postsecondary education and professional success (Goode, 2010b; Jones et al., 2009).

Although technology has been used to facilitate learning among underserved collegians (Palma-Rivas, 2000), students moving from community colleges to four-year institutions may find themselves at a disadvantage compared to peers who began their postsecondary education at four-year institutions and who have established positive technological identities and a high level of comfort with the technology used in university life. Lacking the technological preparation of their peers, students may question their general academic abilities (Goode, 2010a). In response, many colleges and universities have implemented technological literacy requirements, requiring students to demonstrate technological proficiency as part of their general education requirements. These same expectations follow students into their careers as employers place increased emphasis on the need for technology skills (Jones et al., 2009).

ASSESSING TECHNOLOGICAL LITERACY

The responsibility for evaluating student technological literacy, and providing the means to achieve it, is daunting. Few institutions have successfully defined the *technological literacy* needs of their students. The absence of a uniform definition for *technological literacy* confounds the issue, resulting in varied types of assessments, which are shown in Table 4.1. Universities may offer required courses, online help, or noncredit skills training, allowing students to demonstrate their competency or meet the requirement in a number of ways (VanLengen, 2004). Most, however, rely on courses and testing as the primary methods for fulfilling technological literacy requirements.

Although some objective measures of technological literacy exist, many assessments rely on self-perception instruments, as they are generally more applicable across disciplines (van Vliet et al., 1994). Unfortunately, research has shown little agreement between objective tests and self-assessments, leaving one to wonder if self-assessments can be used at all without a validating measure (van Vliet et al., 1994). Students' perceptions of their computer skills are often inflated and at odds with the skill sets employers look for.

Table 4.1
DESCRIPTION OF TECHNOLOGICAL LITERACY ASSESSMENTS

Assessment	Description
Computer ability scale	Objective, 22-item Likert-style survey covering computer ability, software ability, awareness, programming skill, and perceived control (Smith & Necessary, 1996)
Computer literacy courses*	Generally covers basic computer concepts, hardware concepts, and use of productivity software; may also include ethical and societal issues regarding the use of technology (Gaide, 2004)
European Computer Driver's License/International Computer Driver's License (ECDL/ICDL)	Computer-based simulation requiring completion of tasks using Word, Excel, PowerPoint, and Access (Wilkinson, 2006)
Self-assessments*	Generally covers perceived level of competence with computer concepts, hardware concepts, and use of productivity software (van Vliet et al., 1994; Wilkinson, 2006;)
Skills assessment manager	Computer-based simulation requiring completion of tasks using productivity software such as Word, Excel, PowerPoint, and Access; provides student data to inform curriculum decisions (Wilkinson, 2006)

*Institutions may customize the assessments.

Having established a measure of students' technological literacy, college and university leaders must work with employers to determine specific competencies that correspond to institutional requirements, provide for the transfer of skills across courses, improve instruction, and ultimately provide linkages between classroom and workplace use (Hartley, Kinshuk, Koper, Okamoto, & Spector, 2010; Russell, 2003). Faculty can be a valued resource in this process by identifying the particular knowledge, skills, and abilities required to meet specific academic goals (Osika & Sharp, 2002).

FROM TECHNOLOGICAL LITERACY TO
TECHNOLOGICAL FLUENCY

The report *Being Fluent With Information Technology* (NRC, 1999), poses an interesting question: Given the rapid growth of technology and the need to adapt to continual change, is being technologically literate enough?

> To adapt to changes in the technology . . . involves learning sufficient foundational material to enable one to acquire new skills independently after one's formal education is complete. This requirement of a deeper understanding than is implied by the rudimentary term *computer literacy* motivated the committee to adopt *fluency* as a term connoting a higher level of competency. (p. 2; italics added)

This fluency describes a deeper understanding of technology and increasingly skilled use (NRC, 1999). The American Library Association (2001) defined *fluency with technology* as understanding the underlying concepts of technology and applying problem solving and critical thinking in the use of technology. Although the U.S. Department of Education (2010) detailed broad technology goals, it stopped short of defining *technological fluency*. Yet the report underscored the need for students to use information, tools, and technologies effectively, resulting in a commitment to lifelong learning. Similarly, the NRC indicated that true technological fluency allows individuals to adapt to changes in technology and acquire new skills beyond formal education (King, 2007; U.S. Department of Education, 2010).

Today's college graduates must possess "critical thinking, communication, social and computer skills" (King, 2007, p. 61). A survey of employers in Atlanta, Boston, Detroit, and Los Angeles confirmed this, reflecting the need for technology skills. The results "showed that a majority of newly filled jobs for noncollege graduates required computer use on a daily basis, and the figure was even higher, more than 75%, for college graduates" (Wilkinson, 2006, p. 109). Graduates who possess technological fluency, regardless of their discipline, have a competitive advantage in comparison to students who have not mastered basic computing (Compton, Burkett, & Burkett, 2002).

Postsecondary institutions are poised to provide instruction in these critical job skills, yet integrating technology into the curriculum has been a problem because most institutions define computer literacy requirements based on computer skills alone (Wilkinson, 2006). The NRC (2002) noted that colleges tend to view computer literacy as the ability to perform specific tasks using software programs such as those in the Microsoft Office suite. This typically includes tasks like word processing, working with spreadsheets, creating a presentation, or working with a database.

Curricular initiatives such as writing across the curriculum and reading across the curriculum are well documented, but few examples or best practices exist for technology across the curriculum (TAC). The TAC program at George Mason University, developed by Agee and Holisky (2000), is one example of a TAC program with well-defined outcomes, goals for instruction, and detailed competencies for undergraduate students. Holisky (n.d.) detailed 10 technology goals for liberal arts students, with electronic collaboration, electronic document management, and electronic presentations as the top three priorities of TAC. Additional skills include using electronic tools for research and data analysis, using databases to manage information, using spreadsheets, using graphical and multimedia technologies, and having a working knowledge of computer hardware and software. Other TAC programs, such as the one at Oregon State University (n.d.), focus solely on instructional media technologies that are seldom used in the workplace.

INTEGRATING TECHNOLOGY ACROSS THE CURRICULUM

Smith and Caruso (2010) indicated that students want technology integrated in college curricula. In a study of undergraduate students and information technology, students expressed frustration in their survey responses, revealing that faculty and lecturers did not include practical applications of technology in courses (Smith & Caruso, 2010). Likewise, students detailed limited exposure to nonacademic programs such as Microsoft Office, the leading software suite used in the workplace (Smith & Caruso, 2010). Considering these survey responses, academic leaders must address the need for technological competency development in higher education.

Community colleges play an important role in the development of a technologically competent workforce. Yet there are significant challenges to the implementation of curricula that address technological competencies. Students traditionally served by community colleges may still lack a home computer and rely on the college for access to hardware, software, and Internet connectivity (Hagedorn, Perrakis, & Maxwell, 2007). For some, student use of technology could be limited to the capacity and infrastructure of the community college itself.

Community colleges can integrate technology into the curriculum by expanding general education requirements to include technological competencies and by using technology in classrooms to foster technological expertise (Levine, 2002; Zeszotarski, 2000). Integrating technology does not require a complete revision of teaching methods and pedagogy; instructors can start small by providing guided explorations of the Internet, requiring e-mail assignment submissions, and requiring students to use software for in-class presentations (Poynton, 2005). In this regard, faculty must design lessons and assignments that help students develop their technological skills (Kaminski, Switzer, & Gloeckner, 2009). With increased exposure to technology, students will become more proficient and develop enhanced skills (McCoy, 2010). Beyond the efforts of individual instructors, community college leaders should view technological competencies from an interdisciplinary perspective, encouraging the development of these competencies across the curriculum. Skills and competencies acquired through classroom knowledge development can translate to the workplace, as students may use similar skills in workplace contexts (Philip, 2007). One challenge to achieving the integration of technology across the community college curriculum is the technological competency of community college faculty.

Faculty must have professional development opportunities that allow them to enhance their own technological skills to facilitate the growth of those same skills in students. Yet most faculty development opportunities focus on educational media and technology, rather than the technology students need once they leave postsecondary education. At Oregon State University (n.d.), for example, its TAC initiative encourages faculty to integrate educational media and technology into their courses (e.g., clickers, blogs, wikis, and Blackboard course management tools) rather than focusing on the technology that students will encounter in the workplace. Similarly, most scholarly articles on postsecondary faculty development and technology detail attempts to build online teaching competencies for faculty rather than the design of curricula that will build the technological competencies of students (Diaz et al., 2009). With community colleges employing a large number of part-time faculty, community college leaders must address professional development opportunities for adjunct and often transient academic professionals. Part-time faculty have less access to community college infrastructures and computer resources, and full-time faculty have more opportunity to benefit from professional development opportunities (Jackowski & Akroyd, 2010).

In higher education, full- and part-time career and technological education faculty members are uniquely positioned to provide input regarding the

TAC curriculum. Given their close ties to business and industry, these faculty members may be more familiar with technological competencies required in the workplace. Partnerships between community college career and technological education programs and employers could assist students as they develop skills to manage information and use commonly accepted forms of workplace technology (Bragg, 2001; Dellow, 2007). As a result, students can develop an efficacious technological identity, creating academic and professional opportunities throughout their lives (Goode, 2010b).

CONCLUSION

As Poynton (2005) stated, "Colleges and universities are charged with preparing students for professional positions across all disciplines, and have a responsibility to develop computer literacy in their students to provide the skills necessary for employability and lifelong learning" (p. 870). Nowhere is this more important than on community college campuses, where students arrive with diverse skills and diverse motivations for enrolling.

Postsecondary institutional leaders must be sensitive to the digital divide and net generation phenomena and acknowledge that the adoption and development of technological competencies is inconsistent even in subpopulations of community college students. To develop technological fluency in students, community college leaders must identify and define technological competencies and work with faculty to ensure technology integration across the curriculum. Without clearly defined goals for achieving technological fluency, community college students will remain unprepared for the technical demands that await them in the workplace and future learning environments.

REFERENCES

Agee, A., & Holisky, D. (2000). Technology across the curriculum at George Mason University. *Educause Quarterly*, *23*(4), 6–12. Retrieved from http://www.ducause.edu/ero/educause-quarterly-magazine-volume-23-number-4-2000

American Library Association. (2001). Competency standards for higher education. *Teacher Librarian*, *28*(3), 16–22.

Bragg, D. D. (2001). Opportunities and challenges for the new vocationalism. *New Directions for Community Colleges*, (115), 5–15.

Compton, D., Burkett, W., & Burkett, G. (2002). The prediction of perceived level of computer knowledge: The role of participant characteristics and aversion toward computers. *Informing Science, 5*(4), 219–224. Retrieved from http://digilib.unsri.ac.id/download/v5n4p219-224.pdf

Cummings, D., & Buzzard, C. (2002). Technology, students and faculty . . . How to make it happen! *Techniques, 77*(8), 30–33.

Dellow, D. A. (2007). The role of globalization in technical and occupational programs. *New Directions for Community Colleges,* (138), 39–45.

Diaz, V., Garrett, P., Kinley, E., Moore, J., Schwartz, C., & Kohrman, C., II. (2009). Faculty development for the 21st century. *Education Review Online, 44*(3), 46–55. Retrieved from http://www.educause.edu/ero/article/faculty-development-21st-century

Gaide, S. (2004). Are technical skills core competencies? How do we measure them? *Distance Education Report, 8*(22), 5–7.

Goode, J. (2010a). Mind the gap: The digital dimension of college access. *The Journal of Higher Education, 81*(5), 583–618.

Goode, J. (2010b). The digital identity divide: How technology knowledge impacts college students. *New Media Society, 12*(3), 497–513. doi: 10.1177/1461444809343560

Hagedorn, L., Perrakis, A., & Maxwell, W. (2007, Fall). The negative commandments: Ten ways urban community colleges hinder student success. *Florida Journal of Educational Administration and Policy, 1*(1), 25–33.

Hargittai, E. (2010). Digital na(t)ives: Variation in Internet skills and uses among members of the "net generation." *Sociological Inquiry, 80*(1), 92–113. doi: 10.1111/j.1475-682X.2009.00317.x

Hartley, R., Kinshuk, Koper, R., Okamoto, T., & Spector, J. (2010). The education and training of learning technologists: A competencies approach. *Educational Technology & Society, 13*(2), 206–216.

Holisky, D. (n.d.). *Ten IT goals: Information technology goals for liberal arts students.* Retrieved from http://tac.gmu.edu/goals/tenitgoals.html

Jackowski, B., & Akroyd, D. (2010). Technology usage among community college faculty. *Community College Journal of Research and Practice, 34*(8), 624–644.

Jones, S., Johnson-Yale, C., Millermaier, S., & Perez, F. (2009). U.S. college students' Internet use: Race, gender and digital divides. *Journal of Computer-Mediated Communication, 14*, 244–264.

Kaminski, K., Switzer, J., & Gloeckner, G. (2009). Workforce readiness: A study of university students' fluency with information technology. *Computers & Education, 53*, 228–233.

King, B. R. (2007, November 1). Think small! A beginner's guide to using technology to promote learning. *EDUCAUSE Quarterly, 30*(1), 58–61.

Levine, L. (2002, January). *Using technology to enhance the classroom environment. The journal*. Retrieved from http://thejournal.com/Articles/2002/01/01/Using-Technology-to-Enhance-the-Classroom-Environment.aspx

McCoy, C. (2010). Perceived self-efficacy and technology proficiency in undergraduate college students. *Computers & Education, 55,* 1614–1617.

McManus, T. (2006). Assessing proficiencies in higher education. *Community & Junior College Libraries, 13*(3), 43–51.

Messineo, M., & DeOllos, I. Y. (2005). Are we assuming too much? Exploring students' perceptions of their computer competence. *College Teaching, 53*(2), 50–56.

National Research Council. (1999). *Being fluent with information technology*. Retrieved from http://www.nap.edu/catalog.php?record_id=6482

National Research Council. (2002). *Technically speaking: Why all Americans need to know more about technology*. Retrieved from http://www.nap.edu/catalog.php?record_id=10250

Nichols, J. (2010). *Computer literate*. Retrieved from http://astro.temple.edu/~nichols/55c1/sld001.htm

No Child Left Behind Act of 2001, Pub. L. No. 107-110, 107th Cong., 1st Sess. (2002).

Oregon State University. (n.d.). *Technology across the curriculum*. Retrieved from http://oregonstate.edu/tac/

Osika, E. R., & Sharp, D. P. (2002). Minimum technical competencies for distance learning students. *Journal of Research on Technology in Education, 34*(3), 318–325.

Palma-Rivas, N. (2000). Using technology to facilitate learning for minority students. *New Directions for Community Colleges,* (112), 73–83.

Philip, D. (2007). The knowledge building paradigm: A model of learning for net generation students. *Journal of Online Education, 3*(5). Retrieved from http://www.ict-21.ch/com-ict/IMG/pdf_Philip.pdf

Poynton, T. (2005). Computer literacy across the lifespan: A review with implications for educators. *Computers in Human Behavior, 21,* 861–872.

Russell, J. (2003). Making use of the new student assessment standards to enhance technological literacy. *The Technology Teacher, 63*(2), 27–32.

Smith, B. N., & Necessary, J. R. (1996). Assessing the computer literacy of undergraduate college students. *Education, 117*(2), 188–193.

Smith, S., & Caruso, J. (2010). *ECAR study of undergraduate students and information technology*. Retrieved from http://www.educause.edu/Resources/ECARStudyofUndergraduateStuden/217333

Trotter, A. (2009, Winter). Tech literacy confusion: What should you measure? *Education Week's Digital Directions, 2(3),* 20–22.

U.S. Department of Education. (1996). *Getting America's students ready for the 21st century: Meeting the technology literacy challenge.* Washington, DC: Government Printing Office.

U.S. Department of Education. (2010). *National education technology plan 2010. Transforming American education: Learning powered by technology.* Washington, DC: Author.

Vaidhyanathan, S. (2008). Generational myth: Not all young people are tech-savvy. *The Chronicle of Higher Education, 55*(4), B7–B9.

VanLengen, C. A. (2004). *Computer literacy alternatives.* Retrieved from http://franke.nau.edu/images/uploads/fcb/04-10.pdf

van Vliet, P. J. A., Kletke, M. G., & Chakraborty, G. (1994). The measurement of computer literacy: A comparison of self-appraisal and objective tests. *International Journal of Human-Computer Studies, 40*(5), 835–857.

Wilkinson, K. (2006). Students computer literacy: Perception versus reality. *Delta Pi Epsilon Journal, 48*(2), 108–120.

Zeszotarski, P. (2000). *Computer literacy for community college students.* Retrieved from ERIC database. (ED438010)

Part Two

Welcome to Campus
Supporting Today's Community College Learners

THIS SECTION OPENS WITH A CHAPTER by Patricia Munsch and Lisa S. Kelsay regarding the needs and issues of different student populations. More specifically, they share information regarding undocumented students, at-risk students, and international students attending community colleges. Further, this chapter aligns the shifting demographics with the multiple missions of the community college.

Cara W. McFadden and Martha Mazeika present what they consider the critical elements needed for creating effective partnerships between academic and student affairs in community college settings. The chapter highlights the importance of academic and social integration for student success and student development theory as a foundation for collaboration and meeting student learning outcomes.

One means of achieving learning outcomes is through making student transitions and adjustment seamless. The creation and development of programs suited to meet the needs of increasingly diverse students is generating a culture of innovation at community colleges across the country. In addition, to meet the needs of the students, programs are also being created to engage and retain students. Jessica

Hale looks at successful orientation programs and explains why they are effective.

Residence life is one factor that contributes to student persistence and matriculation in many four-year institutions. However, less is known about residential housing on community college campuses. As the number of community colleges with residence life operations increases, research literature regarding best practices in student housing will provide meaningful information for campus leaders for decision making. To situate this issue, Carin W. Barber and Daniel J. Phelan provide an overview of the varied student demographics of community college students who live in, or could benefit from, on-campus housing. In addition, they explore the facilities, staffing, and programming models in place for residence life operations and practical strategies for working with residential populations at community colleges. They also provide action steps for student affairs professionals to consider when developing or managing residential communities at two-year institutions.

5

Who Are Our Students?

Patricia Munsch and Lisa S. Kelsay

W HAT DO Halle Berry, Queen Latifah, Eddie Murphy, Nick Nolte, and Shawntel Smith have in common? Each graduated from a community college. Halle Berry attended Cuyahoga Community College; Queen Latifah, Manhattan Community College; Eddie Murphy, Nassau Community College; Nick Nolte, Pasadena City College; and Shawntel Smith, Westark Community College. Graduates from community colleges go on to careers as bankers, politicians, actors, newscasters, teachers, welders, and automotive technicians, among many other occupations.

In the fall 2011 semester, 13 million students attended 1,132 community colleges, and 41% of those students were enrolled as full-time students (American Association of Community Colleges [AACC], 2013). Of all the undergraduates in the United States, 45% were community college students; 59% of full-time community college students were employed part-time, and 40% of part-time community college students were employed full-time (AACC, 2013). During the 2010–11 academic year, 734,154 associate's degrees and 429,676 certificates were awarded in the United States to community college students (AACC, 2013).

Students choose to attend a community college for many different reasons. For example, Samantha became a student quite by accident—she hopped on the wrong bus one day and it dropped her off at the front door of a community college. As an armed forces veteran and a nontraditional-age student, she had not considered reentering the classroom. She thought she might be too old, and she was not sure if her interests would lead to a career. Like

Samantha, many of the students in community colleges are nontraditional age. The average age of a community college student in 2011 was 28, 15% were age 40 or over, 40% were first generation, and 3% of the student population were veterans (AACC, 2013). Samantha is now a graduate of a community college, pursuing a bachelor's degree in psychology, and completing a study-abroad program in Europe. As for her career, she has many interests and enjoyed all the courses she took at the community college, which made choosing a career difficult.

Chen (2008) cited seven myths surrounding the community college and the students who attend them:

> Myth #1: Students attend community college because they did not get accepted to four-year universities.
> Myth #2: Community colleges are only for people who want a vocational technical job.
> Myth #3: No one successful goes to community college.
> Myth #4: Obtaining a community college degree is not as useful as a university degree.
> Myth #5: Most students who attend community college are older, with full-time jobs.
> Myth #6: It is not easy to transfer from a community college to a four-year university.
> Myth #7: Community college students cannot make it in a four-year university.

Many people believe these statements are accurate. The reality is that students choose to attend community colleges for a number of reasons, including lower tuition, transferability of credits, open admissions, smaller class sizes, closeness to home, and flexibility of school schedule to accommodate work (Chen, 2011; Provasnik & Planty, 2008).

As with any college, students attending community colleges apply for financial aid. In the 2007–2008 academic year, 46% of students received aid (AACC, 2013). The average tuition and fees for the 2012–2013 academic year in a public community college were $3,130, while the average tuition and fees for a four-year public institution were $8,660 (AACC, 2013).

The demographics of students who attend community colleges are all encompassing. When discussing the diversity of community college students, Clark (2012) noted, "The nontraditional community college student is our traditional student" (p. 511). Characteristics commonly defining nontraditional students include "first generation to college, adult student, employed, parent, LGBT [lesbian, gay, bisexual, transgender], veteran, historically underrepresented ethnic groups, and lower socioeconomic status" (Clark, 2012, p. 511). Additional characteristics include low academic achievement and being a returning student. For some of these categories, research is abundant, but others, such as adult learners and veterans, are discussed more in depth in Chapters 9 and 10, respectively.

The scope and purpose of this chapter is to explore the relationships between the myths described by Chen (2008) and specific student populations that are often ignored by the literature but are present on community college campuses. Specifically, the chapter discusses undocumented students, international students, displaced workers, and each population's relationship with community colleges.

STUDENT POPULATIONS

Undocumented students, international students, and displaced workers are not often discussed in the context of community colleges; however, community colleges are called on to meet the needs of these populations. For example, community college staff often provide support to undocumented students in obtaining lawyers to aid in their goal of achieving citizenship, assisting international students with filing their visa paperwork, or serving as mediator between displaced workers and their case managers. All three student populations have increased needs in specific areas that community college personnel are called upon to meet collectively and individually.

Undocumented Students

Twelve million undocumented people are living in the United States (Bacon, 2008; Lopez, 2010; Passel, 2006; Perez, 2009), and an estimated 1.1 million undocumented children under the age of 18 attend school in the United States, about 65,000 of whom graduate from high school each year (Fix & Passel, 2003; Lopez, 2010; Passel & Cohen, 2009; Perez, 2009). It is estimated that 13,000 undocumented high school students continue on to college each year, which represents about 10% to 20% of the undocumented youths who live in the United States (Capps, Fix, Passel, Ost, & Perez-Lopez, 2003; Lopez, 2010; Passel & Cohen, 2009).

Based on the U.S. Supreme Court's decision in *Plyler v. Doe* (1982) undocumented children have the right to education. However, this right ends when they complete high school. Only 16% of undocumented women and 10% of undocumented men ages 18 to 24 enter college after high school (Perez, 2009). The following paragraphs explore the relationship between undocumented students and community colleges in the college choice process, admission process, and subsequent barriers.

Perez (2009) and Lopez (2010) explored the college choice process for undocumented students, and their findings were similar: both found that undocumented students looked for institutions that would admit them, have lower costs, and were located close to their homes and places of work. Based on these criteria, many undocumented students sought out community colleges. Additionally, undocumented students noted that it was important for them to feel they had information regarding the institution including cost, tuition policies, and its approach to undocumented students, and they felt more comfortable with institutions if they could meet members of the faculty or staff before enrolling in courses. Finally, peer and social networks played a part in college choice, as undocumented students were more likely to attend institutions that were attended by friends or relatives (Lopez, 2010; Perez, 2009).

Lopez (2010) found that undocumented students faced a series of barriers in their admission to four-year institutions and were unable to fully complete admission applications because of their lack of an international student visa or Social Security number. Not wishing to reveal their status through an admission application, they were unable to complete the process. Because of these challenges, undocumented students often choose community colleges, which tend to have more lenient admission requirements and lower overall costs (Lopez, 2010).

Undocumented students face additional challenges because of tuition differentials and financial aid issues (Szelenyi & Chang, 2002). *Tuition differentials* refers to the higher tuition rates paid by certain populations of students on college campuses, including out-of-state and undocumented students. Currently, 18 states have provisions for undocumented students to be assessed in-state tuition rates so that they paid the same tuition for their education as their local native-born peers (National Conference of State Legislatures, 2014). Rincon (2008) examined the challenges of implementing tuition subsidies for undocumented students. The research demonstrated that in the 10 states that do provide in-state rates, a series of ongoing barriers were still in place. These barriers included highly organized public advocacy groups that continue to bring lawsuits against the provisions of in-state tuition to undocumented students. Finally, there was a backlash of hostility from various anti-immigration groups that posed a threat to undocumented students on campus. Such threats include revealing undocumented students' status to federal immigration officers, public slurs on campus, and protests and marches. For undocumented students in those 10 states that provided subsidies, there was still potential for fear regarding their legal status.

Because of these factors, undocumented students have been more likely to attend community colleges than any other form of higher education (Horwedel, 2006). In a study of Texas community colleges, researchers examined undocumented students in the context of the community college system and found that the number of undocumented students in community colleges increased once undocumented students paid only the in-state tuition rate (Jauregui, Slate, & Stallone-Brown, 2008). Szelenyi and Chang (2002) found access and tuition were the leading reasons immigrant students chose community colleges, and the second important factor was their limited educational attainment and achievement.

As the undocumented population of students enroll on public community college campuses, staff members must be cognizant of the delivery of services. Given the scrutiny surrounding undocumented students, information must be made available in a nondisclosure format, such as the college website, so that undocumented students can access information without revealing their status to college officials. Institutional leaders should clearly identify the tuition policies of the state community college system for undocumented students and provide information on how to apply to the institution and for the in-state tuition rates (where applicable). Finally, when possible community college faculty and staff should provide mentors and support groups for undocumented students to share resources and provide a stronger connection to peers and the institution.

International Students

The population of international students attending community colleges in the United States is growing. According to the Institute of International Education (2011), 87,997 international students were studying in community colleges in 2010–2011, an increase of 6,128 from the 2004–2005 academic year. The international student population expressed interest in studying at community colleges because of the low-cost tuition, small class sizes, and individualized attention (McVeigh, 2007).

A study conducted by Mamiseishvili (2012) found that international students selected two-year colleges based on a series of factors, including the location of the institution and the desire to live and attend school in large urban areas rather than rural areas. The students also cited low cost and curricular options as reasons for attendance. The students noted that offering career and transfer paths in the curriculum were a positive attribute of the community colleges. Community colleges often have a strong English-as-a-second-language curriculum that enrolls a number of international students (Kisch, 2012).

International students also cited the open-access policies of community colleges as a reason for attendance. International students with either low or no Test of English as a Foreign Language scores looked to community colleges as an entrance point into the U.S. system of higher education (Kisch, 2012). As Hulstrand (2009) documented, international students often start in a community college for the purpose of language acquisition course work. However, once within the system, international students gain insight into the opportunities offered by the transfer process and continue their course work in the community college. Once they have completed their general education course work, they transfer to baccalaureate programs.

Despite the growing population of international students on community college campuses, many institutions have yet to provide outreach or services for them; as a result, persistence of international students is a problem (Raby, 2007). One of the key performance indicators for international student persistence in community colleges is their relationship with faculty and academic advisers. Students who felt they had strong relationships with faculty or academic advisers were more likely to persist to graduation (Mamiseishvili, 2012).

International students have unique challenges in the enrollment process. First, there are no similar models internationally, so they may not understand the opportunities connected with a community college education (Kisch, 2012). Second, once enrolled, international students may face challenges regarding tuition costs, which are usually higher for out-of-county residents. Third, as many community colleges do not provide housing, international students who choose community colleges must also find suitable housing arrangements (Kisch, 2012).

Community college leaders need to recognize the value of involving international students as members of their campus communities. Through dedicated recruitment and scholarship opportunities, community college personnel would be able to increase this student population on their campuses. Once on campus this population should be provided with additional guidance and support regarding visa requirements, language, and culture acquisition, along with assurance of basic needs such as housing. By embracing and fostering this growing population on campus, community college campuses benefit financially and culturally. The population brings a diverse background and perspective to the campus and infuses a global perspective in classes.

Displaced Workers

The mission of community colleges includes workforce development and economic transformation (Schwitzer, Duggan, Laughlin, & Walker, 2011). Because of the economic downturn, this aspect of the community college mission has become more relevant with an increase in the number of displaced workers, which are individuals who have involuntarily and permanently lost their job through the closing of a place of employment or elimination of their position. The U.S. Bureau of Labor Statistics (2012) reported that 56% of displaced workers will continue to be unemployed for 15 weeks postemployment, and that 41% of these individuals will remain unemployed for a full year. Displaced workers tend to come from office positions, service positions, or manufacturing positions (U.S. Bureau of Labor Statistics, 2012).

Community colleges play a vital role in retraining displaced workers, and many institutions work with the federal government through the transitional adjustment assistance programs, which provide services and financial support to displaced workers (Schwitzer et al., 2011). Because of the growing population of displaced workers, questions arise regarding their acculturation to college and the impact of their new training. Owen and Fitch (2003) studied the career concerns of displaced workers and found that students were interested in two major aspects of career planning. They wanted assurance that they were choosing careers that met their skill sets and that employment opportunities would be available to them in their chosen fields. Schwitzer et al. (2011) examined the adjustment of displaced workers to community colleges. The results of the study indicated that these students had social adjustment experiences similar to those of their peers. The displaced workers had stronger grade point averages than their peer group, and they reported higher levels of academic adjustment.

Administrators of community college campuses must ensure that displaced workers are taught academic skills and provided with the career, financial, and personal counseling necessary to reenter the workforce. Baird (2011) reported on a process to understand the projected needs for employment skills from prospective employers. Upon the completion of a yearlong study, institutional leaders devised 13 new career programs suited to meet the needs of local businesses and displaced workers. Students were referred to the program through a number of different venues. The program improved job placement and provided upward mobility for individuals currently employed. This is a strong example of the purposeful approach institutional leaders can implement when working to serve displaced workers. In addition to providing a true connection to employer-sought job skills, community college personnel must provide the academic support for displaced workers to be successful. This includes services such as free tutoring offered at varying times, in-depth career counseling, and financial and personal support.

CONCLUSION

Community college campuses now include more and more distinct student populations. Through the open-access mission, low-cost tuition, various curricular options, small class sizes, and expanded support services, community colleges continue to appeal to diverse populations. Undocumented students, international students, and displaced workers are all found on our campuses, yet the research is limited on the relationship between each group and community colleges. It is critical for faculty, staff, and administrators to embrace the growing diversity on our campuses and thoughtfully approach ways to support the specific needs of each group.

As stated earlier, there is a series of myths regarding the reasons students choose to attend community college. The reality is far more complex. Students enroll in community colleges with varied backgrounds. Undocumented students need to keep their legal status undisclosed, and the bureaucracy of community college admissions must be easier to navigate than four-year institutions. International students need access to language acquisition course work and college-level courses concurrently. Displaced workers need to re-create their professional identities. We cannot simply list the reasons why students choose to enter our institutions; we need to recognize the unique and diverse backgrounds of our students, listen to their needs, and find the best ways to contribute to their success.

REFERENCES

American Association of Community Colleges. (2013). *2013 community college fast facts*. Retrieved from http://www.aacc.nche.edu/AboutCC/Documents/FactSheet2013.pdf

Bacon, D. (2008). *Illegal people: How globalization creates migration and criminalizes immigrants.* Boston, MA: Beacon Press.

Baird, D. (2011). Improving and communicating workforce skills: A regional initiative. *Community College Journal of Research and Practice, 35,* 595–607.

Capps, R., Fix, M., Passel, J. S., Ost, J., & Perez-Lopez, D. (2003). *A profile of the low-wage immigrant workforce* (Issue Brief No. 4). Washington, DC: Urban Institute Immigration Studies Program.

Chen, G. (2008). *The top 7 community college myths.* Retrieved from http://www .communitycollegereview.com/articles/8

Chen, G. (2011). *Why more students are choosing community colleges over traditional four-year schools.* Retrieved from http://www.communitycollegereview.com/ articles/361

Clark, L. (2012). When nontraditional is traditional: A faculty dialogue with graduating community college students about persistence. *Community College Journal of Research and Practice, 36,* 511–519.

Fix, M., & Passel, J. S. (2003). *Immigration: Trends and implications for schools.* Washington, DC: Urban Institute Immigration Studies Program.

Flores, S. M., & Chapa, J. (2009). Latino immigrant access to higher education in a bipolar context of reception. *Journal of Hispanic Higher Education, 8*(1), 90–109.

Horwedel, D. M. (2006). For illegal college students, an uncertain future. *Diverse Issues in Higher Education, 23*(6), 23–26.

Hulstrand, J. (2009). International students at community colleges. *International Educator, 18*(3), 94–98.

Institute of International Education. (2011). *Open doors 2011 report on international education exchange: Enrollments by institutional type.* Retrieved from http:// www.iie.org/en/Research-and-Publications/Open-Doors/Data/International-Students/Enrollment-by-Institutional-Type

Jauregui, J. A., Slate, J. R., & Stallone-Brown, M. (2008). Texas community colleges and characteristics of a growing undocumented student population. *Journal of Hispanic Higher Education, 7,* 346–355.

Kaushal, N. (2008). In-state tuition for the undocumented: Education effects on Mexican young adults. *Journal of Policy Analysis and Management, 27*(4), 771–792. doi:10.1002/pam.20366

Kisch, M. (2012). Recruiting international students—community college style. *International Educator, 21*(3), 52–59.

Lopez, J. K. (2010). *Undocumented students and the policies of wasted potential.* El Paso, TX: LFB Scholarly Publishing.

Mamiseishvili, K. (2012). Academic and social integration and persistence of international students at U.S. two-year institutions. *Community College Journal of Research and Practice, 36*(1), 15–27.

McVeigh, P. (2007). Community college: A world of opportunities. *Education USA Connections, 1*(3), 2–3.

National Conference of State Legislatures (2014). *Undocumented student tuition: State action.* Retrieved May 27, 2014 from http://www.ncsl.org/research/education/undocumented-student-tuition-state-action.aspx

Owen, T. R., & Fitch, T. J. (2003). Career concerns of displaced workers in vocational training. *Community College Journal of Research and Practice, 27*(3), 191–201.

Passel, J. S. (2006). *The size and characteristics of the unauthorized migrant population in the U.S.: Estimates based on the March 2005 current population survey.* Washington, DC: Pew Hispanic Center.

Passel, J. S., & Cohen, D. (2009). *A portrait of unauthorized immigrants in the United States.* Washington, DC: Pew Hispanic Center.

Perez, W. (2009). *We are Americans: Undocumented students pursuing the American dream.* Sterling, VA: Stylus.

Plyler v. Doe, 457 U.S. 202 (1982).

Provasnik, S., & Planty, M. (2008, August). *Community colleges: Special supplement to the condition of education 2008.* Washington, DC: National Center for Education Statistics.

Raby, R. L. (2007). Internationalizing the curriculum: On- and off-campus strategies. *New Directions for Community Colleges,* (123), 57–66.

Rincon, A. (2008). *Undocumented immigrants and higher education: Si se puede!* New York, NY: LFB Scholarly Publishing.

Schwitzer, A. M., Duggan, M. H., Laughlin, J. T., & Walker, M. A. (2011). Community college adjustment among dislocated workers. *Community College Journal of Research and Practice, 35,* 645–666.

Szelenyi, K., & Chang, J. C. (2002). ERIC review: Educating immigrants: The community college role. *Community College Review, 30*(2), 55–73.

U.S. Bureau of Labor Statistics. (2012). *Household data annual averages. Table 29. Unemployed persons by reason for unemployment, sex, age, and duration of unemployment.* Retrieved from http://www.bls.gov/cps/cpsaat29.pdf

6

Academic and Student Affairs Collaboration

A Value for Student Success in the Community College Environment

Cara W. McFadden and Martha Mazeika

I N 2010 THE AMERICAN ASSOCIATION OF COMMUNITY COLLEGES (AACC, 2010) reported active involvement in working with lawmakers, policy developers, and many other stakeholders to develop legislation that supports two-year colleges' investment in student success. The involvement was prompted by President Barack Obama's proposal to invest $12 billion in community colleges to increase graduation rates over the next decade (AACC, 2010). Academic transfer, vocational technical education, continuing education, developmental education, and community service are the discipline areas that direct the mission of community colleges (Cohen & Brawer, 2008). Collaboration among these disciplines is key to student success in all areas served by the community college. Collaboration must also occur among the different sectors (academic affairs, student affairs, workforce development, and developmental education) of the community college (Keeling, 2004).

With continued competition for resources and growth of college campuses, partnerships between academic and student affairs are crucial; the challenge is determining strategies to achieve student success. Many staff and faculty at institutions of higher education (two-year, four-year, public, private) are striving to find ways to enhance student success on their campuses. They independently create what they believe is the best approach to improve student success. However, instead of collaborating to achieve a shared goal, many departments on campuses across the country fail to work together to find solutions. The answer is to integrate collaborative program initiatives, instead of separate agendas for students, that enhance the student learning experience as well as contribute to overall success (Keeling, 2004, 2006).

Creating a commitment to the educational mission of the college (Goldstein & Thorp, 2010) supports collaboration efforts between academic and student affairs. Support and guidance from institutional leaders, educators, and student affairs professionals must be deliberate to discover ways they can work together to create challenging experiences for students while providing appropriate support that will contribute to student achievement and success (Evans, Forney, Guido, Patton, & Renn, 2010).

This chapter highlights critical elements needed for creating effective partnerships between academic and student affairs in the community college setting. We define and explain *student success* and the relationship of social involvement and support systems. Through implications of practice, we describe the importance of student development theory as a foundation for collaboration. Understanding the whole student and how students develop during their time in college is imperative for academic and student affairs staff. We explore aspects of student engagement in and outside the classroom and how these experiences lead to success or failure in the community college environment. We explain the importance of shared responsibility among academic and student affairs staff in relation to student success. Specific approaches for constructing strong partnerships between academic and student affairs for community college environments are presented.

STUDENT SUCCESS

In 2010 about 21 million students entered postsecondary degree-granting institutions, and about 7 million students were enrolled in two-year institutions (National Center for Education Statistics [NCES], 2011). Researchers have attempted to identify factors related to students' success (McConnell, 2000). For example, Cohen and Brawer (2008) discussed recruitment, orientation, and specifically involving students in campus activities, such as counseling and advising, career counseling, and other nonclassroom activities, as factors of success. In comparison, the Integrated Postsecondary Education Data System measures success by first-year retention rates and graduation rates (NCES, n.d.). Kuh, Kinzie, Buckley, Bridges, and Hayek (2007) defined *student success* as "academic achievement; engagement in educationally purposeful activities; satisfaction; acquisition of desired knowledge, skills, and competencies; persistence; and attainment of educational objectives" (p. 10). By this definition, student success is the responsibility of academic and student affairs; however, during the development of student success measures, the values of academic and student affairs administrators may vary. Student success is influenced by a student's social integration and involvement during his or her college experience. Student support systems are an integral part of student success; however, multiple factors contribute to the students' experiences. For the purposes of this chapter, these definitions are applicable to support and define collaborative efforts between academic and student affairs. Each definition is an explanation of what defines success, such as data, program, services, skills, and competencies.

Involvement

One contributor to student success is social involvement. Involvement in college varies among student populations. Mutter (1992) studied student persistence at community colleges and found that students "reported less social than academic links to the college" (p. 314). In addition, the study concluded "there are differences between the persistence of students who talk with college employees about school and career issues and information matters [and] those who do not" (p. 314). Students who had already selected a career prior to entering the institution were more likely to persist (Mutter, 1992). These results explain the need for involvement in career counseling and advising for students without a clear career choice.

Female students are more likely to make friends on campus, study with other students, and meet in study groups for a particular course (Hagedorn, Maxwell, Rodriguez, Hocevar, & Fillpot, 2000) than male students. Yet community college students overall are less likely to participate in the college's social groups or clubs than students at four-year colleges and are even less likely to attend one of the college's cultural events. They tend to come to campus for class and then leave (Miller, Pope, & Steinmann, 2005). In addition, college life events did not receive high ratings on the Likert scale according to a study by Miller et al. (2005), who concluded that community colleges need to create an environment that encourages involvement.

Support Systems

A study by Miller et al. (2005) found community college students consult with family members, not peers or community college personnel. Community college students need to receive support from people inside and outside the college. These students need to be encouraged to interact with peers and know that college administrators can be a key factor in achieving academic success. Pacheco (1994) said that college should be a social setting where students feel supported and comfortable, which leads to student involvement. How students integrate themselves into college and the support they receive are predictors of student persistence.

Students also have support from programs and orientation courses. A study by Derby and Smith (2004) concluded that students who enrolled in an orientation class at a community college had higher rates of retention and comfort levels with campus life. Kanter (2010) highlighted a study completed by the Community College Research Center that reported student success can be achieved by aligning programs that support student success with the institution's policies and procedures. Regardless of whether it is a program or college policy that helps increase success, it is necessary to understand that community college environments are unique. Community colleges serve the community in transfer and vocational education (Cohen & Brawer, 2008). Large populations of students are placed in developmental education courses in the hope they will transfer to college-level courses. In addition, community college administrators focus programs on veterans, first-generation students, adults, and other at-risk populations with the goal of student success. Part Three of this book contains additional information on these populations.

To begin collaboration efforts, academic and student affairs professionals should be aware of their colleges' missions and values as they develop program initiatives. It is also important that they understand there are a variety of individual factors (e.g., background characteristics of students, academic or social involvement, integration of experience) that may hinder or facilitate student success.

FRAMEWORK MODELS

Astin's model studies college effects through the function of inputs, environment, and outcomes and highlights the institutional environment as it offers opportunity; however, students also guide their own growth by taking an active role in the environment (Astin, 1977). According to Tinto's (1993) model of institutional departure, students need to deal with academic and social integration in order to succeed.

Pike, Kuh, and Gonyea (2003) conducted a study to investigate the influence of institutional mission, student involvement, and outcomes on student learning. Their conceptual model proposed that background characteristics of the student, college environment, academic involvement, social involvement, and integration of experiences influence student learning (i.e., student success). The change process students go through depends on the unique characteristics of the individual student and all stakeholders (faculty, staff, advisers, peers) in the college environment. Understanding the college environment assists faculty and staff in effecting change and promoting student success.

COLLABORATION

AACC (2005) highlights six competencies, one of which is collaboration: "An effective community leader develops and maintains responsive, cooperative, mutually beneficial, and ethical relationships that nurture diversity, promote the success of all students, and sustain the community college mission" (p. 3). Developing collaboration efforts between student affairs and academic affairs might start with small projects, conversations, or sharing of ideas. Although the different focuses of academic affairs (student learning) and student affairs (student development) might hinder collaboration (Kezar & Lester, 2009), student learning is a shared responsibility. Keeling (2006) provides a contextual method for academic and student affairs to communicate effectively with one another about student learning. Collaborative initiatives must start with building relationships that will lead to partnerships on projects.

STUDENT DEVELOPMENT THEORY FOUNDATION

The foundation for supporting academic and student affairs partnerships is understanding student development theory (SDT), which creates a basis for understanding college students during their time in the university setting. Collaborations between faculty and student affairs staff can enhance the student learning experience by acknowledging where students are in their development (Evans et al., 2010). SDT is an influential factor that enables student affairs professionals and faculty to "identify and address student needs, design programs, develop policies, and create healthy college environments that encourage positive growth in students" (Evans et al., 2010, p. 7).

SDT provides faculty and student affairs administrators with a theoretical explanation for student behavior. Although faculty and staff who choose to use SDT as a foundation for developing collaborative programs for students may encounter opposition from those who choose to dismiss the theory as useless (Evans et al., 2010), faculty and staff are responsible for creating educational opportunities for their colleagues that enhance their understanding of SDT. SDT is a viable approach in that it assists faculty and staff to understand that each student is unique in relation to his or her intellectual and social abilities as well as his or her identity (e.g., race, ethnicity, gender, sexual preference). Through SDT, educators and staff have the opportunity to create collaborative efforts for diverse student populations that engage them in holistic learning environments.

Prior to implementing collaborative programs and initiatives, faculty and student affairs staff need to have a common language when using SDT. The partnership between academic and student affairs staff should be grounded in linking theory to practice. SDTs are typically grouped into three areas: psychosocial, cognitive-structural, and typology. Psychosocial theory states that development occurs throughout an individual's life span based on the individual's personal experience as well as his or her interpersonal life. Cognitive-structural theory focuses on the way individuals process their thoughts but not what they actually think. Typology theories are not strictly developmental, such as psychosocial and cognitive theories, but typology assists in the understanding that there are distinct individual differences (e.g., personality, learning preferences, interests, abilities) in college students' mental processing (Evans et al., 2010).

To link these theories to practice, student affairs professionals could use the practice-to-theory-to-practice (PTP) model, an 11-step process with five overarching components: practice, description, translation, prescription, and practice (Knefelkamp, Golec, & Wells, 1985). In summary, (a) concerns and desired goals are determined, (b) theories that link to the desired goal and analyze student characteristics as well as the college environment are investigated, (c) factors that create a balance of challenge and support for the student or student population are identified, (d) goals are evaluated and programs created, and (e) programs are implemented and assessed and changes are made as needed (Knefelkamp et al., 1985).

The PTP model is one practical way to employ SDT to create a challenging and supporting environment for students during their time in college. Creating environments, which develops students, makes SDT imperative when constructing partnerships between academic and student affairs. SDT must be regarded as a holistic approach to student growth and less as a linear progression (Evans et al., 2010). Leaders of academic and student life departments in the college play a vital role in the development and success of students. SDT provides stakeholders with the relevancy of developmental stages of college students and support for strategically aligning program outcomes that contribute to a student's overall success at the university.

IMPLICATIONS FOR PRACTICE: PARTNERSHIPS FOR STUDENT SUCCESS

Interest in improving academic and student affairs partnerships at colleges has increased across the country (American College Personnel Association, 1994; Keeling, 2006; Kezar, 2003b; King, 1999). With the demand to increase graduation rates at community colleges, more of a focus on developing these partnerships in two-year institutions is needed.

Partnerships between academic and student affairs staff can enable more students to be successful during their time at two-year institutions. One approach is setting a foundation with theory to assist faculty and staff in understanding how students are uniquely different from one another. Another is facilitating student engagement in and outside the classroom by illustrating to students that there is a unified mission to challenge and support them during their experience. The third approach is modeling shared responsibility to enhance relationships on campus as well as make better use of resources that academic and student affairs may misuse. Collectively, these three approaches provide multiple opportunities for everyone involved to contribute cooperatively to student success.

Setting the Foundation With SDT

Learning experiences that assist student affairs professionals in understanding how students are unique can be used in the community college environment to help create a foundation with SDT. For example, administrators can ask their staff to participate in a book club—for example, staff are grouped into teams that read a book related to college student development. Each team (book club) is composed of four to five staff members who read the same book and create a lesson to present at a future staff meeting or retreat. A second example is student organization observations in which staff members select a student organization on campus (a group that is out of one's area of responsibility) to observe during the semester. From the observation, the staff members write a reflection and relate their observations to SDT. The observation experiences can then be discussed with colleagues during a staff training or designated workshop. For a faculty experience, college administrators can develop an SDT scholar initiative. The faculty group would consist of 10 to 12 faculty who study SDT for a semester typically, it is beneficial to involve multiple disciplines—mathematics, science, business, and so on—as a collective learning process on how to use SDT as well as to learn about student affairs resources on campus. To be successful partners, faculty and staff need to take advantage of opportunities to learn about SDT and of applying theory to practice.

Facilitating Engagement In and Outside the Classroom

The Community College Survey of Student Engagement (CCSSE) was established in 2001 on the premise of *student engagement*, defined as "the amount of time and energy that students invest in educationally meaningful activities" (McClenney, 2006, pp. 47–48). The five benchmarks are active and collaborative learning, student effort, academic challenge, student-faculty interaction, and support for learners (McClenney, 2006). Added to Tinto's (1993) model of institutional departure, these benchmark areas help develop programs and interventions that may result in students staying at the institution.

Although academic and student affairs educators use different means to engage students, their goals are "unifying—for students to learn, grow, and become engaged" (Riera, 2010, p. 19). Student engagement is a dual responsibility. Harper and Quaye (2009) argued that we rely heavily on students to take full responsibility for becoming involved in the college environment. However, educators and administrators should be held accountable for fostering conditions that enable students to be involved (Harper & Quaye, 2009).

As stated previously, the CCSSE has a benchmark that focuses on student-faculty interaction and support for learners (McClenney, 2006). It is essential for faculty and student affairs staff to create program initiatives together in and outside the classroom that support interaction with students and different learning styles. Inviting a staff member from the career-advising office to an undergraduate class session on writing résumés and cover letters is a great example of collaboration. By doing this, a support system for the students is created with academic and student affairs.

Each year, the Center for Community College Student Engagement (2009, 2010) publishes findings of its survey administered in the spring. The 2009 findings, focused on campus connections, reported the importance of connecting students in and outside the classroom, especially support services such as tutoring and advising. In the report, data showed that perceptions of support services are important to faculty and students alike, but a low percentage of students use the services. Examples of how colleges are increasing connections on campus include programs to increase student participation in activities, mandatory orientation programs, and peer tutoring. The report on the 2010 findings focused on student success and completion. Learning communities served as successful tools for deeper learning, especially those that integrated support services into the course work. Along with student programs (advising, orientation, tutoring, and learning communities), early intervention programs, service-learning, academic bridge programs, distance education programs, and conflict management services are examples of collaboration opportunities for student affairs and academic affairs (Dale & Drake, 2005).

Modeling Shared Responsibility

To be effective, faculty, staff, and students must share responsibility for educational quality and student success. Above all, faculty and student affairs staff must consider how each department in the college setting reflects and supports the educational mission of their institution (Kuh, Kinzie, Schuh, & Whitt, 2005). In addition, a review of policies, programs, practices, and staff who have contact with students must be undertaken to identify how they reflect and support students' learning and success. A review of stakeholder (academic affairs, student affairs, faculty, staff, administrators, and students) values is imperative to understand the lens each group uses to view student learning and success (Kuh et al., 2005). All members of the college community should be seen as educators responsible for student success and learning (Keeling, 2006).

One example of shared responsibility is an administrator-facilitated training session for staff and faculty to understand different aspects and roles of the departments on campus. During a professional development program called Learning College Day at a suburban community college in the Midwest, a presentation called "Cake, Coffee, and Collaboration" describes what faculty, administrators, and staff do on a daily basis (Mazeika & Lezon, 2011). The conversation resulted in a better understanding of and respect for the multiple positions on college campuses, from campus operations workers to faculty members to counselors to directors in student affairs. In addition, coming together to create opportunities for dialogue builds relationships that lead to collaborative program initiatives that enhance student success.

CONCLUSION

Two-year college administrators are encouraged to implement approaches to develop strong programs, policies, and practices that promote student learning and success on campus. Our review of academic and student affairs partnerships is just the beginning for enhancing student success at two-year institutions. Acknowledging SDT assists faculty and staff in better understanding our diverse student populations. By understanding our students, we are more equipped to provide collaborative initiatives that enhance student engagement in and outside the classroom as well as create supportive experiences that contribute to student success. Strong faculty and student affairs professionals understand the importance of shared responsibility and of developing the whole student. It is imperative for higher education professionals to identify with institutional strategic priorities and align those priorities in the creation of opportunities that contribute to student success.

Over the next decade, academic and student affairs collaboration will be even more important as institutions continue to be held accountable for student success. Leaders throughout campuses will be successful only if they seek out strategies for change by targeting organizational barriers that hinder potential collaboration (Kezar, 2003a). Determining barriers on campus may contribute to thriving academic and student affairs collaboration and "create seamless learning environments" (Kezar, 2003a, p. 20). Engaging in discussions with partners, implementing programs, and assessing collaboration efforts will be a continuous undertaking for administrators to create learning environments that challenge students academically and provide opportunities for growth and development. Faculty and staff members' ability to collaborate will better equip students with meaningful educational opportunities as well as prepare them for life after graduation.

REFERENCES

American Association of Community Colleges. (2005). *Competencies for community college leaders*. Washington, DC: Author.

American Association of Community Colleges. (2010). *2010 fact sheet: Building a nation of learners by advancing America's community colleges*. Washington, DC: Author.

American College Personnel Association. (1994). *The student learning imperative: Implications for student affairs*. Washington, DC: Author.

Astin, A. W. (1977). *Four critical years*. San Francisco, CA: Jossey-Bass.

Center for Community College Student Engagement. (2009). *Making connections: Dimensions of student engagement (2009 CCSSE findings)*. Austin, TX: Author.

Center for Community College Student Engagement. (2010). *The heart of student success: Teaching, learning, and college completion (2010 CCSSE findings)*. Austin, TX: Author.

Cohen, A. M., & Brawer, F. B. (2008). *The American community college* (5th ed.). San Francisco, CA: Jossey-Bass.

Dale, P. A., & Drake, T. M. (2005). Connecting academic and student affairs to enhance student learning and success. *New Directions for Community Colleges*, (131), 51–64. doi:10.1002/cc.205

Derby, D. C., & Smith, T. (2004). An orientation course and community college retention. *Community College Journal of Research and Practice, 28*, 763–773.

Evans, N. J., Forney, D. S., Guido, F. M., Patton, L. D., & Renn, K. A. (2010). *Student development in college: Theory, research, and practice* (2nd ed.). San Francisco, CA: Jossey-Bass.

Goldstein, B., & Thorp, H. (2010, August 29). How to create a problem-solving institution. *The Chronicle of Higher Education*. Retrieved from http://chronicle.com/article/How-to-Create-a/124153/

Hagedorn, L. S., Maxwell, W., Rodriguez, P., Hocevar, D., & Fillpot, J. (2000). Peer and student-faculty relations in community colleges. *Community College Journal of Research and Practice, 24*, 587–598. doi:10.1080/10668920050139730

Harper, S. R., & Quaye, S. J. (2009). *Student engagement in higher education: Theoretical perspectives and practical approaches for diverse populations*. New York, NY: Routledge.

Kanter, M. (2010). Rethinking student affairs: Today's students need more directive support. *NASPA Leadership Exchange, 8*(1), 16–21.

Keeling, R. P. (Ed.). (2004). *Learning reconsidered: A campus-wide focus on the student experience*. Washington, DC: National Association of Student Personnel Administrators and American College Personnel Association.

Keeling, R. P. (Ed.). (2006). *Learning reconsidered 2: Implementing a campus-wide focus on the student experience.* Washington, DC: American College Personnel Association, Association of College and University Housing Officers International, Association of College Unions International, National Academic Advising Association, National Association for Campus Activities, National Association of Student Personnel Administrators, National Intramural-Recreational Sports Association.

Kezar, A. (2003a). Achieving student success: Strategies for creating partnerships between academic and student affairs. *NASPA Journal, 41*(1), 1–22.

Kezar, A. (2003b). Enhancing innovative partnerships: Creating a change model for academic and student affairs collaboration. *Innovative Higher Education, 28*(2), 137–156.

Kezar, A. J., & Lester, J. (2009). *Organizing higher education for collaboration: A guide for campus leaders.* San Francisco, CA: Jossey-Bass.

King, P. (1999). Improving access and educational success for diverse students: Steady progress but enduring problems. In C. S. Johnson & H. E. Cheatham (Eds.), *Higher education trends for the next century: A research agenda for student success* (pp. 5–12). Washington, DC: American College Personnel Association.

Knefelkamp, L. L., Golec, R. R., & Wells, E. A. (1985). *The practice-to-theory-to-practice model.* Unpublished manuscript, University of Maryland, College Park.

Kuh, G. D., Kinzie, J., Buckley, J. A., Bridges, B. K., & Hayek, J. C. (2007). Piecing together the student success puzzle. *ASHE Higher Education Report, 32*(5).

Kuh, G. D., Kinzie, J., Schuh, J. H., & Whitt, E. J. (2005). *Assessing conditions to enhance educational effectiveness: The inventory for student engagement and success.* San Francisco, CA: Jossey-Bass.

Mazeika, M. P., & Lezon, L. (2011, March). *Cake, coffee, and collaboration.* Presentation for the meeting of Learning College Day, Moraine Valley Community College, Palos Hills, IL.

McClenney, K. M. (2006). Benchmarking effective educational practice. *New Directions for Community Colleges,* (134), 47–55.

McConnell, P. J. (2000). ERIC review: What community colleges should do to assist first-generation students. *Community College Review, 28*(3), 75–87.

Miller, M. T., Pope, M. L., & Steinmann, T. D. (2005). Dealing with the challenges and stressors faced by community college students: The old college try. *Community College Journal of Research and Practice, 29,* 63–74.

Mutter, P. (1992). Tinto's theory of departure and community college student persistence. *Journal of College Student Development, 33,* 310–317.

National Center for Education Statistics. (2011). *Digest of education statistics: List of tables and figures.* Retrieved from http://nces.ed.gov/programs/digest/2011menu_tables.asp

National Center for Education Statistics. (n.d.). *About IPEDS*. Retrieved from http://nces.ed.gov/ipeds/about/

Pacheco, A. (1994, Fall). Bridging the gaps in retention. *Metropolitan Universities*, 5(2), 54–60.

Pike, G. R., Kuh, G. D., & Gonyea, R. M. (2003). The relationship between institutional mission and students' involvement and educational outcomes. *Research in Higher Education*, 44, 241–261.

Riera, J. (2010). Engaging pedagogy: One student's lesson in teaching and learning. *About Campus*, 15(3), 17–21. doi:10.1002/abc.20021

Tinto, V. (1993). *Leaving college: Rethinking the causes and cures of student attrition* (2nd ed.). Chicago, IL: University of Chicago Press.

7

Student Orientation at Community Colleges

Jessica Hale

T HE LANDSCAPE OF HIGHER EDUCATION is changing. More students than ever are enrolled in higher education in the United States (National Center for Education Statistics, 2008). In fact, community college enrollment has increased fivefold since 1965 (Rosenbaum, Deil-Amen, & Person, 2006). Along with this expansive growth, the range of diversity among the students served by community colleges has broadened.

The creation and development of programs suited to meet the needs of increasingly diverse student populations is generating a culture of innovation and a hotbed of creativity at community colleges across the country. Born from necessity, programs aimed at increasing student retention and successes are emerging nationwide. Spurred on by initiatives like Achieving the Dream, community college faculty and administrators are now examining achievement gaps at their institutions and crafting programs and services designed specifically to engage and retain these students from day one (Rutschow et al., 2011). It should come as no surprise then that orientation programs designed to help students integrate academically and socially into the institution are becoming an area of institutional focus. They are usually the primary point of contact for students beginning their postsecondary education and as such present a unique opportunity for institutions to begin increasing student persistence.

This chapter discusses the role of orientation in student development, the emergent nature of orientation programs at community colleges, the organizational context for orientation departments, and the sources of orientation funding. Additionally, the rise of mandatory orientation programs, the development of these programs for special populations, the creation of online orientation resources, and the increased professionalism of orientation staff are addressed. By examining these trends, the evolving nature of orientation programs at community colleges can be better understood.

ORIENTATION AND STUDENT DEVELOPMENT

Orientation at its core is an opportunity for student development. Chickering and Reisser (1993) identified seven vectors of psychosocial development in students: developing confidence (intellectual, physical, and interpersonal), managing emotions, moving through autonomy toward interdependence, developing mature interpersonal relationships, establishing identity, developing purpose, and developing integrity. These vectors relate to the six typical content areas of an orientation program identified by Smith and Brackin (2003):

1. *Academic information*: academic structure, guidelines, regulations, class scheduling, meeting faculty and deans, exposure to live or simulated classes
2. *General information*: campus tours, international policies and regulations, available services, campus history and traditions
3. *Logistical concerns*: financial aid, business matters, registering a car, getting an identification card or library card, and purchasing books
4. *Social and interpersonal development*: campus activities, clubs and events, social activities, group- or team-building exercises, and getting acquainted exercises
5. *Testing and assessment*: placement tests, attitudinal tests, career and personality tests, and demographic surveys
6. *Transitional programming*: workshops about career development, commuting, or affective issues such as fears, anxiety, and relationships

In addition to their seven vectors of student development, Chickering and Reisser (1993) also identified the following environmental factors that influence student development: institutional objectives, institutional size, friendships and student communities, recognition of and respect for individual differences, student-faculty relationships, curriculum, teaching, acknowledgment of the cyclical nature of learning and development, student development programs and services, and integration of work and learning. These factors of influence are particularly relevant to the discussion of emerging orientation trends.

The first environmental factor identified by Chickering and Reisser (1993), institutional objectives, means the "clear and specific objectives to which personnel pay attention and use to guide the development of programs and services" (p. 40). For a growing number of community colleges, the objective is to increase retention and promote student success, although the means to achieve this may vary (Kuh, Kinzie, Schuh, & Whitt, 2010). The increasing recognition that orientation programs promote retention, and thus the institutional objectives, may account for the increasing number of orientation programs at community colleges throughout the country. The diversity of the organizational structure in where orientation programs fit in the context of their organizations, and the funding directed toward the program, reflects how the institution plans to achieve its objectives.

The second environmental factor, institutional size, suggests that for meaningful student development to occur, students must have opportunities to participate in campus life and experiences that promote satisfaction (Chickering & Reisser, 1993). As community colleges are often commuter schools with fluid entry points (i.e., open enrollment, rolling admissions, and varied course lengths rather than a 15-week term), involving students in meaningful participation in campus life could be a challenge. As a result, many institutions are requiring participation in orientation as a primary campus life experience.

Another environmental factor, friendships and student communities, is the institution's ability to provide students with the opportunity to interact with other students, collaborate, develop a reference group, and be introduced to people from diverse backgrounds (Chickering & Reisser, 1993). As primarily open admissions institutions, community colleges may have less control over their incoming student populations than a selective four-year institution, but the opportunities to help students develop friendships and communities still exist. Orientation programs foster interaction and collaboration among new students. Furthermore, orientation programs targeting special populations (e.g., traditional-age students, nontraditional students, dually enrolled high school students, transfer students, veterans, international students, and English-as-a-second-language students [ESL], to name a few) can help students identify reference groups and build a community on their first day on campus. Special population orientations also address another environmental factor—recognition of and respect for individual differences—by adjusting program content, delivery, and communications to address the needs of these different student populations.

Student-faculty relationships, curriculum, and teaching are other environmental factors core to student development. Providing students with the opportunity to interact with faculty and prepare for college instruction and delivery is a key component of orientation programs. Until recently, this preparation occurred in a strictly face-to-face format. However, dramatic changes in the landscape of higher education have changed this paradigm. In fall 2010, more than 6.1 million students were enrolled in at least one online course, an increase of more than half a million from the previous year (Allen & Seaman, 2011). This shift to an online format means that influential factors like student-faculty relationships, teaching, and curriculum are occurring in more than one medium. As a result, some institutions are developing online orientation resources for all students to prepare them for college instruction and delivery online. This adaptation is an acknowledgment of the cyclical nature of learning and development, another environmental factor that can influence student development.

Additionally, student development programs and services play an influential role in student development. Chickering and Reisser (1993) recommended "that administrators of student programs and services redefine themselves as educators and refer to themselves as 'student development professionals'" (p. 278). This shift in identity may result in increased professionalism of orientation staff at community colleges. Additionally, as a growing number of current students are asked to work or volunteer in orientation programs, community colleges are addressing another key environmental factor in promoting student development: integration of work and learning.

THE NATURE OF ORIENTATION AT COMMUNITY COLLEGES

Not all community colleges currently offer orientation programs; however, a growing number are beginning to offer them as a means to increase retention. In a study conducted in the state of Michigan, only 15 of 21 community colleges offered an orientation of some kind (Robinson, Travis, Stryker, & Hancock, 2009). Although this number is roughly 70%, evidence from Hale and Timmerman (2011) suggests that the percentage of community colleges offering orientation programs may be larger. At an extended session on community college orientation at the 2011 National Orientation Directors Association conference, 28 of the 29 institutions represented offered an orientation program.

The format of orientation programs at community colleges varies more than that of four-year institutions. For example, some community colleges offer orientation once per term, while others offer sessions multiple times a week, or they offer online versions available 24 hours a day. Additionally, there is variation in the length of these programs whether or not they are mandatory, address specific populations, or have different formats (online versus face-to-face).

Also, structures vary significantly among community colleges. These variations allow the institution to align services, departments, and individual positions with the college's vision and philosophy. Likewise, orientation programs are very rarely organized in the same fashion from institution to institution. In some cases, orientation functions as a separate department, whereas in others it is treated as a job responsibility for a specific position or for multiple positions. Furthermore, orientation programs may be integrated into a variety of other departments, such as admissions or enrollment, student activities, or student support services.

For example, at Washtenaw Community College in Michigan, orientation is a separate department under the umbrella of the Support Services and Student Advocacy Division, functioning with one full-time orientation manager, two part-time employees, and a work-study student (Hale & Timmerman, 2011). At Lone Star College in Texas, rather than being a separate department, orientation is housed under Student Outreach and Retention. Orientation programs at Lone Star are run with 2 full-time staff members, 10 full-time and part-time advisers, 8 counselors, and 4 student workers (Hale & Timmerman, 2011). At Massachusetts Bay Community College, orientation is a part of the Student Development Office employing a full-time coordinator, dean of students, administrative assistants, and 8 to 10 orientation leaders to facilitate orientation programs (Hale & Timmerman, 2011). At Monroe Community College in New York, orientation is part of the Office of Student Life and Leadership Development. The assistant director of the department, with the help of a support staff member and 13 peer mentors (Hale & Timmerman, 2011), coordinates this program.

Although the variations among colleges can pose a challenge when looking for information from peer institutions, they also provide a rare opportunity in higher education: the opportunity to break away from tradition. The variations in the structural alignment and organization of orientation programs at community colleges can be viewed as experiments, the results of which can provide administrators of other institutions with creative solutions on how best to align their orientation programs with their unique organizations while maximizing resources.

ORIENTATION FUNDING

Historically, student affairs programs have been viewed as ancillary to the core function of the college and as a result are often the first programs to be reduced or cut in a time of fiscal trouble. Because orientation programs are typically located in the Division of Student Affairs, a reduction in funding for these programs can be a common problem for two-year and four-year institutions. To address this fiscal instability, many of the faculty and staff involved in orientation programs at the community college are trying to make these programs self-sustaining.

One method for sustainability that is gaining traction is instituting an orientation fee. An orientation fee is a set amount that students are required to pay the college to participate in orientation activities. For example, Tyler Junior College in Texas has a $50 student orientation fee that is used to offset orientation costs (A. Lewis, personal communication, March 14, 2011). If the orientation program is mandatory for new students, then this becomes a mandatory fee.

Another emerging trend for orientation departments seeking fiscal independence is to develop cost-sharing partnerships. Many orientation departments solicit funds and materials from other units on campus as well as outside entities to defray operational costs. At Tallahassee Community College in Florida, the student government association funded orientation (E. Clark, personal communication, March 4, 2011). Cost-sharing partners may also provide materials at no charge, such as handbooks, notebooks, and pens. One company, All By Student Notebooks, provides thousands of free spiral-bound notebooks to new students at community colleges across the country by selling advertising space on the notebooks. Orientation program staff may also collaborate with local businesses in return for the opportunity to advertise to the new student audience. Lansing Community College in Michigan is able to fund a yearly planner for students using this model (A. Calhoun, personal communication, April 17, 2013).

A final method to foster self-sustainability is to reduce existing costs. In many cases, this means moving activities that required traditional paper products to digital online forums. For example, Massachusetts Bay Community College has replaced paper registration with an online orientation sign-up. In addition, the student handbook and orientation presentation, typically printed and provided to students in face-to-face orientation programs, are being put online for students to download and print at home as needed (C. Mack, personal communication, January 6, 2012). Flyers and postcards are being replaced by e-mails and social networking applications like Facebook and Twitter. Lone Star does not participate in any mailings but rather uses e-mail for confirmation letters and phone calls for reminders. Additionally, the college relations department updates the college Facebook page with new student orientation information (C. Timmerman, personal communication, January 6, 2012). Reducing costs may also require creative staffing and using more student leaders and paid professionals already on campus for orientation functions. In tight financial times, creative solutions like these are becoming increasingly necessary.

THE RISE IN MANDATORY ORIENTATION

As is evident from the programs of the latest Achieving the Dream 2011 Strategy Institute Conference (2011) and the National Orientation Directors Association conference (2010, 2011), mandatory orientation programs are growing areas of interest at community colleges. The introduction of a mandatory entrance requirement, such as orientation, has been controversial in light of the traditional open-access admission philosophy of community colleges. However, evidence suggests that participation in orientation increases persistence from term to term.

In a study conducted at Big Bend Community College in Washington, the persistence (from the fall 2008 semester through the winter 2009 semester) for students who attended a fall orientation program was 21% higher than for students who did not attend (Bauer, Lacher, & Zavala-Lopez, 2011). This was also true across ethnicities (Latino, 19%; White, 23%; other, 17%; Bauer et al., 2011). Although orientation at Big Bend Community College is not required, these findings support the notion that student retention is positively influenced by participation in orientation and strengthens the argument that orientation should be mandatory for all students.

Mandatory orientation programs are becoming more popular across the nation (Cuevas & Timmerman, 2010). Two-year institutions in California, Colorado, Florida, Indiana, Kentucky, Massachusetts, Michigan, Missouri, New York, and Texas have already adopted mandatory orientation programs (Hale & Timmerman, 2011). Ivy Tech Community College in Indiana implemented a mandatory in-person orientation and noted a higher persistence rate (statistically significant at the 99% confidence level) for students who attended orientation versus students who did not attend (DeWeese, 2011). For the fall 2010 cohort, of the 6,619 students who attended an in-person orientation, 5,134 students persisted into spring 2011 (about 78%). Of the 4,585 students who did not attend orientation, only 3,311 persisted to spring 2011 (about 72%; DeWeese, 2011).

Yakima Valley Community College in Washington also implemented a mandatory orientation program as well as an admissions deadline (Bauer et al., 2011). The retention rates from fall to winter for students from the 2004–2006 cohorts (before these changes were implemented) to the 2007–2009 cohorts (the latest cohort after these changes were implemented) demonstrated that these policies positively affected retention. Specifically, retention rates improved 4% for Whites, 5% for Latinos/Hispanics, 7% for Asians, 8% for African Americans, and 15% for Native Americans. These results indicate that mandatory orientation (in combination with an admissions cutoff date) may be an even greater benefit for minority students.

The results of the national Survey of Entering Student Engagement (2008) are also of interest. Although 54% of community college students surveyed nationwide indicated they did not attend an on-campus orientation at their institutions, they "consistently recommended mandatory orientation" (p. 9). This finding suggests that students understand the value of attending orientation even if they are not aware of its impact on persistence. As such, implementing mandatory orientation programs is likely to add value to the student experience even if the results are not easily measured by enrollment and graduation rates.

ORIENTATION FOR SPECIAL POPULATIONS

Another trend in community college orientation is the creation of special programs for student subgroups that allow institutions to "tailor programming to meet the needs of the students being served . . . [and increase] student interaction (with others in similar circumstances) . . . [as well as] engagement through relevant programming and information sharing" (Cuevas & Timmerman, 2010, pp. 73–74). Colleges that develop custom orientation programs for subgroups of their populations may be better prepared to help facilitate academic and social integration (Tinto, 1993).

Common special populations for orientation programming include traditional-age students, nontraditional-age students, dual-enrolled high school students, transfer students, veterans, developmental students, international students, and ESL students. Dozens of community colleges nationwide currently offer some kind of special population orientation (Hale & Timmerman, 2011).

Institutions may offer more than one special population orientation. For example, Washtenaw Community College offers four different in-person student orientation programs (traditional students, nontraditional students, ESL students, and foreign students with F1 visas). Although Washtenaw has not tracked the impact of these special orientation programs on retention, orientation manager Cristina Buzas reported that student feedback indicated that students value having information tailored to their needs as well as meeting people with similar interests (C. Buzas, personal communication, March 7, 2011).

CREATION OF ONLINE ORIENTATION

Community colleges are leaders in higher education when it comes to the use of technology (Stoik, 2001). In terms of orientation, this means the integration of an online orientation component. Just as with traditional in-person orientation programs, online orientation is used to introduce students to institutional vocabulary, prepare students for registration, acquaint students with the campus layout and resources, and define expectations for technology use and applications at the college (Miller & Pope, 2003). Online orientation is not clock bound, offers easier personal customization, and provides a larger bank of immediately accessed resources through hyperlinks and multimedia than can be provided using in-person group orientation formats.

Online orientation takes a variety of formats. Typically, these programs are offered preorientation, as a replacement for in-person orientation, or as a hybrid of the two (Adams, Granholm, & Hale, 2010). Online orientation can take place synchronously, with participants and facilitators engaging in real time, or asynchronously, in which the exchange of ideas and interaction between participants and facilitators does not occur at the same time. As with traditional face-to-face orientation programs, online orientation may be required or optional. In several cases, online orientation programs are required only for a subgroup of the student population (e.g., traditional students, nontraditional students; Adams et al., 2010).

Research related to online orientations at community colleges is scant, but there is some research on identifying quality components in an online orientation for a community college. In a qualitative study, Hale (2009) used focus groups of students who had completed an online orientation to determine quality components. A total of 44 students participated (27 traditional, 17 nontraditional) in nine focus groups ranging in size from three to seven people. Overall, students identified interactive and customized experience as two important quality components. Further thematic analysis revealed that traditional students were also concerned with the entertainment value of the online orientation and level of detail provided in the content areas (e.g., step-by-step instructions were desired). Nontraditional students, on the other hand, identified flexibility (in terms of access and completion times) and simplicity (ease of use) as two important quality components in online orientation (Hale, 2009).

The popularity of online programs is growing. They not only reduce staffing costs as well as wear and tear on facilities, but also provide a more time-effective option for students seeking entrance at institutions with rolling admissions. Two-year institutions currently using some form of online orientation (mandatory or optional) can be found coast to coast (Hale & Timmerman, 2011).

Additionally, in Robinson and colleagues' (2009) study of 21 Michigan community colleges, 10 (about 67%) considered online orientation mandatory. As the number of institutions developing online orientation programs continues to grow, community colleges are well positioned to provide information on a variety of best practices to various types of institutions.

INCREASED PROFESSIONALISM OF ORIENTATION STAFF

Another notable trend in community college orientation programs is the increased professionalism of orientation staff. More than ever, orientation programs are managed and facilitated by individuals who have graduate degrees. Specifically, many orientation professionals have pursued graduate degrees in student affairs, counseling, or higher education. This level of professionalism of orientation staff increases the legitimacy and credibility of orientation programs.

At the community college, most faculty members in traditional academic disciplines are required to have master's degrees in their areas of specialization. This benchmark of legitimacy is an important cultural element, and extending this same benchmark to orientation staff may reduce the pervasive divide between faculty and staff on campus. Furthermore, mutual respect between faculty and orientation staff may encourage more faculty participation in orientation and increase the number of collaborative efforts between units on campus.

In addition to higher educational levels, orientation professionals are increasingly engaged in professional organizations. The National Orientation Directors Association (NODA, 2009) fosters a network among its members specifically aimed at two-year colleges that promotes sharing best practices and research from institutions across the nation. From 2008 to 2009, the membership of this network doubled (NODA, 2009). Furthermore, orientation professionals from two-year colleges are increasingly featured as authors in NODA's *Journal of College Orientation and Transition* and the joint monograph with the National Resource Center for the First-Year Experience.

This increased professionalism also extends to student leaders. Many community colleges are training current and returning students as orientation facilitators, peer leaders, tour guides, and ambassadors for their orientation programs (Cuevas & Timmerman, 2010). The training for these roles may be limited or extensive, spanning the course of multiple semesters. Furthermore, student orientation leaders may be paid for their efforts, elevating the role from volunteer to paid employee. Community college students are also starting to participate in professional organizations, such as NODA, at the regional and national levels.

Ivy Tech Community College begins recruiting potential student leaders directly from high school. According to assistant vice chancellor for student affairs Sam DeWeese, students are recruited and invited to participate in a half-day interview process that includes group activities and leadership games (S. DeWeese, personal communication, March 4, 2011). Current student leaders as well as advisers then select students to take part in the program, and those selected to be leaders participate in a weeklong intensive training session as well as ongoing training throughout the year of their appointment. These student leaders are paid based on their performance in the program and their scholastic performance (bonuses and any pay cuts are based on grade point average). These students are also expected to participate in NODA conferences at the regional and national levels (S. DeWeese, personal communication, March 4, 2011).

The increased professionalism of orientation professionals may elevate the status of orientation from fluff to substance in the minds of skeptics. At the very least, this change directly benefits students whose first point of contact at the college is a well-informed, well-prepared individual.

CONCLUSION

The landscape of higher education is changing and so too are orientation trends and practices. The social and academic integration of community college students is a primary function of orientation programs across the nation. However, the means to achieve this varies considerably. This chapter discusses the role of orientation in student development and the nature of community college orientation programs. Based on the identified trends, the following are recommendations for practice:

- Align orientation programs to maximize resources and efficiency in the unique organizational context of the institution.
- Develop self-sustaining orientation programs to insulate orientation from decreases in institutional funding.
- Require mandatory orientation programs to increase student success and persistence.
- Tailor orientation programs to meet the academic and social needs of special student populations.
- Create customized and interactive online orientation resources to help students make the transition into the college culture while reducing staffing costs and decreasing the time from orientation to enrollment.
- Define orientation as a college-learning environment and support professional development for community college orientation staff (including student employees).

These recommendations are based on changes already under way in orientation programs at community colleges around the nation. When examined as a whole, these trends portray the changing nature of community college orientation as well as the exciting future of this field.

REFERENCES

Achieving the Dream 2011 Strategy Institute Conference. (2011, February). Conference proceedings of the 2011 Achieving the Dream Strategy Institute, Indianapolis, IN.

Adams, C., Granholm, K., & Hale, J. A. (2010, December 3). *Building the foundation of an effective online orientation* [Webinar]. National Orientation Directors Association and Innovative Educators. Retrieved from http://www.innovativeeducators.org/product_p/656.htm

Allen, I. E., & Seaman, J. (2011). *Going the distance: Online education in the United States.* Retrieved from http://sloanconsortium.org/publications/survey/going_distance_2011

Bauer, K., Lacher, C., & Zavala-Lopez, M. (2011, February). *Welcoming incoming students with an eye on first quarter and first year persistence.* Presented at a meeting of the Achieving the Dream Strategies Institute, Indianapolis, IN.

Chickering, A. W., & Reisser, L. (1993). *Education and identity* (2nd ed.). San Francisco, CA: Jossey-Bass.

Cuevas, C., & Timmerman, C. (2010). Community college orientation and transition programs. In J. A. Ward-Roof (Ed.), *Designing successful transitions: A guide for orienting students to college* (3rd ed., pp. 61–78). Columbia, SC: National Resource Center for the First-Year Experience and Students in Transition.

DeWeese, S. (2011, November). *Mandatory orientation for community college is not a breeze, but it works . . . and we have data.* Presented at the 34th annual conference of the National Orientation Directors Association, New Orleans, LA.

Hale, J. A. (2009, November). *Assessing online orientation: What works for students?* Presented at the 32nd annual conference of the National Orientation Directors Association, Anaheim, CA.

Hale, J. A., & Timmerman, C. (2011, October). *Everything to everyone: The unique challenge of orientations at community colleges.* Presented at the 34th annual conference of the National Orientation Directors Association, New Orleans, LA.

Kuh, G. D., Kinzie, J., Schuh, J. H., & Whitt, E. J. (2010). *Student success in college: Creating conditions that matter.* Retrieved from http://books.google.com/books?id=hLlzNUegXu0C

Miller, T. M., & Pope, M. L. (2003). Integrating technology into new student orientation programs at community colleges. *Community College Journal of Research and Practice, 27*(1), 15–23.

National Center for Education Statistics. (2008). *Digest of educational statistics, 2008.* Washington, DC: Author. Retrieved from http://nces.ed.gov/pubsearch/pubsinfo.asp?pubid=2009020

National Orientation Directors Association. (2009, October). *Board report.* Anaheim, CA: Author.

National Orientation Directors Association. (2010, November). Conference proceedings at the 32nd annual conference of the National Orientation Directors Association, St. Louis, MO.

National Orientation Directors Association. (2011, October). Conference proceedings at the 33rd annual conference of the National Orientation Directors Association, New Orleans, LA.

Robinson, R., Travis, K., Stryker, A., & Hancock, B. (2009, March). *Exploring online orientation programs in Michigan community colleges.* Paper presented at a meeting of the Eastern Michigan University Graduate Student Research Fair, Ypsilanti, MI.

Rosenbaum, J. E., Deil-Amen, R., & Person, A. E. (2006). *After admission: From college access to college success*. New York, NY: Russell Sage Foundation.

Rutschow, E. Z., Richburg-Hayes, L., Brock, T., Orr, G., Cerna, O., Cullinan, D., Kerrigan, M. R., . . . Martin, K. (2011). *Turning the tide: Five years of achieving the dream in community colleges*. New York, NY: MDRC.

Smith, R. F., & Brackin, R. K. (2003). Components of a comprehensive orientation program. In J. A. Ward & C. Hatch (Eds.), *Designing successful transitions: A guide for orienting students to college* (2nd ed., pp. 39–53). Columbia: University of South Carolina, National Resource Center for the First-Year Experience and Students in Transition.

Stoik, J. (2001). Technology's role in collaboration. *Community College Journal of Research and Practice, 25*(1), 37–44.

Survey of Entering Student Engagement. (2008). *Imagine success: Engaging entering students*. Austin, TX: University of Texas at Austin Community College Leadership Program.

Tinto, V. (1993). *Leaving college: Rethinking the causes and cures of student attrition* (2nd ed.). Chicago, IL: University of Chicago Press.

8

Residence Life at Community Colleges

Building New Opportunities for Student Learning

Carin W. Barber and Daniel J. Phelan

S TUDENT HOUSING AND RESIDENCE LIFE PROGRAMS were once found almost exclusively at four-year institutions; however, an increasing number of community colleges now offer on-campus housing for students. This chapter describes the characteristics and unique needs of the community college residential student population. Such an investigation must begin by suggesting that it is unwise to develop community college residential programs that are simply a graft of residential programs at baccalaureate-granting institutions. Although established models may have some similarities among universities, the student population demographics, expectations, and characteristics differ substantially between baccalaureate-granting and associate's degree–granting institutions. As the number of community colleges that provide on-campus living options to students continues to grow, there is a greater urgency to identify best practices in student housing.

More specifically, the need for meaningful research to explore the rationale for pursuing housing at community colleges as well as current operational methodologies, financial structuring, and overall effectiveness is essential. Such literature situated in the community college context is scarce; however, this area is ripe for student affairs professionals to conduct applied research to determine promising operating procedures and solve practical problems (Bers & Calhoun, 2002). Given that residence halls are key environments for broad student learning (Brower & Inkelas, 2010; Longerbeam, Inkelas, & Brower, 2007), such information would ensure a higher likelihood of student success as well as help limit problems in creating a residential program.

The American Association of Community Colleges (AACC, 2013) lists 1,132 community colleges, 986 of which are public, 115 are independent, and 31 are tribal institutions. According to the AACC data analysis of the Integrated Postsecondary Education Data System, 295 (nearly 25%) offer on-campus housing funded by the community college as an option for students (R. Tekle, personal communication, April 17, 2013). The residential population at community colleges is composed of a wide array of students including international, out of state, out of district, athletes, single parents, married, and students with children; indeed, it is a heterogeneous population reflective of the student diversity found in community colleges (Cohen & Brawer, 2008; Levinson, 2005; Williams, 2002). These data, combined with limited available research regarding student housing, support the need for a review of current practice.

FRAMEWORK FOR EXAMINING RESIDENCE LIFE AT COMMUNITY COLLEGES

The Center for Community College Student Engagement's (CCCSE, 2010a, 2010b) *The Heart of Student Success* explored students' educational experiences at institutions that grant associate's degrees and detailed how they can strategically enhance learning, focusing on faculty-student relationships at community colleges. In this section, we address how each of the four strategies to "promote learning and college completion" (CCCSE, 2010b, p. 2) can apply to the residential setting and provide recommendations for practice. The specific strategies outlined in *The Heart of Student Success* are (a) strengthen classroom engagement, (b) integrate student support into living and learning experiences, (c) expand professional development focused on engaging students, and (d) create policy conditions to promote learning and completion (CCCSE, 2010a, p. 8; CCCSE, 2010b, p. 2). Using these four strategies, we investigated specific ways that residential programs (i.e., on-campus housing) can enhance student learning, and by extension student success, at institutions that grant associate's degrees. Additionally, strategies are suggested to augment faculty-student relationships and bolster student learning in a community college residential context.

Strengthen Classroom Engagement

One measure to strengthen classroom engagement is promoting *deep learning*, defined as "broadly applicable thinking, reasoning, and judgment skills—abilities that allow individuals to apply information, develop coherent world views, and interact in more meaningful ways" (CCCSE, 2010b, p. 2). This definition promotes the consideration of formal as well as informal (e.g., cocurricular, social, and practical) college experiences, which could include campus housing life.

Staff members working with residential programs have the opportunity to promote deep learning, especially among disparate groups (CCCSE, 2010b). The consideration of different races and ethnicities, religions, genders, or political views is an example of what the report identified as deep learning. The residential population at most community colleges is diverse, as is the overall student population (Cohen & Brawer, 2008; Levinson, 2005; Williams, 2002). Students come from a wide array of backgrounds, characteristics, and interests, and opportunities to interact with those who are different are abundant.

For most residential students, campus residence living is the first opportunity to be removed from the familiar structures of living at home with family members and other familiar environments. Consequently, students necessarily become engaged in self-management, decision making, personal agency, social interactions, and resultant cocurricular learning. It is important that administrators not leave to chance that residential students will interact with others or that deep learning will occur. Indeed, Schroeder, Mable, and associates (1994) noted that college leaders should not forego their responsibilities of establishing educational objectives, providing planned learning experiences, and evaluating learning outcomes. In taking these steps, the approach to learning in student housing should be innovative, intentional, interactive, and even structured, and should not be left to drift into a distraction from student learning.

Ideally, deep learning should be at the forefront of administrators' planning efforts for a community college residential program. Further, it is advisable that a focused discussion take place among residence life staff and campus leaders to outline certain ways for the institution to promote and sustain deep learning. Specific examples could include

◆ hiring a diverse residence hall staff (full-time professionals and paraprofessional staff such as resident assistants);
◆ designing experience programs that provide students with the opportunities to imagine an issue from another's perspective;

- providing dedicated learning spaces in the facility, such as computer labs, group meeting rooms, and quiet study areas;
- aiding students in the formation of study groups or learning cohorts;
- establishing linkages between the student housing learning objectives and those of the college's degree outcomes as well as educational planning goals;
- implementing a residence life social program with activities that are deployed on a regular (i.e., calendar-scheduled) basis;
- establishing specific learning programs at the residences such as a green program that includes creating and maintaining a residence vegetable garden, monitoring energy consumption in the building, or implementing a building recycling program;
- encouraging student participation in the operations of the college, such as serving on college operational committees, student groups, and community service activities;
- offering classes or workshops in the residence setting; and
- providing opportunities for student reflection.

The report also cited the need to "build and encourage relationships among students, faculty and staff" (CCCSE, 2010b, p. 2). There are several ways to enhance relationships among students, faculty, and staff in the residential context. Relationship building can occur in the traditional sense by inviting faculty and staff to the residence halls to participate in student life activities in addition to encouraging virtual opportunities (e.g., Twitter, Facebook) for faculty and staff to interact with residential students. Structured interaction (online and face-to-face) is important and takes time and resources to implement. For example, a faculty member could hold office hours in a residence hall for one week a month to establish rapport and meet students face-to-face and then be available for virtual office hours for the remaining weeks. This suggestion is manageable for a faculty member's schedule yet provides personal contact for a student. With so many college students heavily engaged in virtual communities, including social media, online contexts can be a central element in the strategy for promoting deep learning.

Developing appropriate and meaningful ways for faculty and staff to be involved with residential students in person and in virtual communities offers strong possibilities for building relationships. Undoubtedly, strengthening classroom engagement is also critical to student success. Residential staff can support efforts inside and outside the classroom by providing intentional programs that build relationships among students, faculty, and staff

(CCCSE, 2010a). Indeed, staff could actively seek to participate in other campus governance committees or faculty committees to aid in their understanding as well as take advantage of an opportunity to provide input in the development of instructional programming for housing.

Another strategy for strengthening instructional connection and classroom engagement is incorporating classroom facilities in the design of residential facilities. The on-site academic classroom in a residence hall is a powerful means for bolstering classroom engagement, bringing faculty members into the residential environment, and creating a seamless learning environment for students living on campus. As an example of a successful program, Jackson College in Michigan, a rural community college of about 10,000 students, began student housing in 2007 with its first unit designed as a learning community, apartment-style building. The facility includes a computer lab, group study areas, and Internet access throughout. The college's second residential building, constructed in 2009, is certified in Leadership in Energy and Environmental Design (a set of rating systems for green buildings), and it improved on the first design with the addition of a traditional classroom and other informal learning spaces. Jackson College has a third residential facility on its campus master plan that proposes other innovations in student learning, including instructional technologies, learning studios, a hospitality management learning lab, and peer tutoring suites. This particular project is advancing because of increasing costs of higher education combined with student interest in having an on-campus experience.

College planners need to contemplate the impact of the additional facility requirements necessary to meet state and local building codes when considering instructional spaces in a student residential environment. Numerous organizations, including the Society for College and University Planning, provide resources to assist community colleges in considering design elements that promote and support learning for existing and new student housing. Additionally, an increasing number of private providers assist higher education institutions with feasibility analysis, planning, facility design, financing, and operational management. These organizations have emerged and grown to support the increasing number of community colleges adding housing to their campus environments. One of the latest and more significant developments in student housing involves the state of Massachusetts. According to an article in the *Washington Post*:

> The Massachusetts Board of Higher Education approved a policy change . . . that allows the state's 15 community colleges to propose building residence

halls, lifting a ban on such housing that has been in place since 1980. . . . The board believes that this makes Massachusetts the 40th state to permit dorm building on community college campuses. (Johnson, 2013, para. 3)

Integrate Student Support Into Living and Learning Experiences

The second strategy identified to promote learning and college completion on community college campuses is integrating student support into learning experiences (CCCSE, 2010a, 2010b). This particular approach explores how to interweave student support services (e.g., academic advising, career planning, tutoring) into the residential experience to provide a seamless learning environment that integrates services with instructional efforts (Cohen & Brawer, 2008). Once initiated, these support services should include planning elements for sustainability and assessment metrics to determine their relative efficacy.

Freshman seminars intentionally integrate student support into learning experiences and aid in the transition to the college setting. Because support is infused into course work, the model alleviates barriers, such as a lack of awareness of services or a perceived stigma attached to certain support services, which may prevent students from using the services (CCCSE, 2010a). Administrators on a community college campus with residential facilities can intentionally assign students living in a residence hall as a cohort in a freshman seminar class and use residential classroom space, if available. Jackson College has created such a living/learning community where participation in a freshman seminar and an orientation program is mandated. Resident students represent a logical cohort of students called, appropriately, a *learning community*. The college also is preparing to offer other cohort-based classes, such as college orientation, and supplemental instructor-based classes, such as English composition and foundation study courses. Other examples of the living/learning concept in a community college setting include those at Fort Lewis College in Colorado and Jamestown Community College in New York.

With the intersection of learning and living provided by campus housing, students are more likely to be successful in college and persist from term to term (Braxton & McClendon, 2001–2002). Indeed, students living on the community college campus provide a natural opportunity for the college to involve students in enhancing the effectiveness of college by encouraging their participation in college committees. In doing so, administration, faculty, and staff experience firsthand the views and needs of the students they serve. Furthermore, their participation in committee work will likely result in better outcomes that are intended to better serve students. Programs like Jackson College's freshman seminar learning communities connect students in the academic and residential settings, facilitating building relationships, peer support, and social integration. The following sections detail practical considerations, based in the literature, for educational leaders who aim to integrate student support into living and learning experiences at community colleges.

Barriers to integrating services cited by students. According to *The Heart of Student Success* report (CCCSE, 2010a), students cited a lack of awareness of services, a lack of knowledge of how to access services, inconvenience, and a stigma associated with using services as barriers that prevented them from ultimately using services. Mindful of the existence of these challenges, community college educators must strategize on how to design services in a residence hall facility to

- promote awareness of student and academic support services through orientation efforts, regular communications, and marketing as well as special information sessions;
- ensure that residence life staff have proper training in identifying student educational and life challenges so that they are equipped for working with residence students to seek out appropriate services;
- educate the student population on how to access services through tours and the introduction of key resource people to residents;
- enhance convenience for residents through bringing some services to the housing units (such as academic advising, tutoring, supplemental instruction financial aid, counseling services; Levinson, 2005); and
- reduce feelings of stigma associated with accessing services, in part through encouraging conversations with peers who have successfully accessed support systems.

Though convenience is one of the benefits of an on-campus residence hall, its pronounced benefit is its significance in overall student success. Residential life programs can support the academic mission of the community college by offering academic and student services in the residence facilities. Ultimately, residence life staff should regularly assess the needs and interests of the residents through focus groups, surveys, social media, and floor meetings to respond with solution sets and services that continue to develop the residence community and help advance student learning (Williams, 2002).

Using CCCSE data as a guide for choosing services to incorporate into residence halls. Residential facilities at community colleges offer unique opportunities for these institutions to bring services to students. However, determining which services to provide in a residence hall is a decision that requires thoughtful consideration and a review of best practices and available data. The CCCSE, modeled after the National Survey of Student Engagement (2014), is one measure of student engagement. Data from the 2010 CCCSE report (2010a) indicated that community college students viewed the following services as most important: academic advising (64%), career counseling (51%), skill labs (45%), and peer or other tutoring (40%).

Student and academic services, such as academic advising, tutoring, and writing labs, made available in a residential facility can be structured in a manner that serves students and takes into account various staffing patterns. For example, based on staffing and budgets, academic services can either be provided on an ongoing basis or offered during critical times during the semester (e.g., registration periods, beginning or end of the semester, midterms). In some instances, the services could be made available on an on-call basis.

CCCSE (2010a) data illustrate that students view academic advising as highly important, yet students are not connecting with their academic advisers as frequently as desired by the student and institution. Thirty-four percent of CCCSE respondents reported they rarely or never used academic advising or planning services (CCCSE, 2010a). Strategic planning on the part of residence life staff and academic advising can result in enhanced convenience and greater awareness of the importance of academic advising as a student support. By enhancing the visibility of academic advising and bringing the service to the students, college officials can take steps to encourage all students to access the resources available.

Cross programming: Providing multiple student services in the residence halls. The CCCSE (2010a) data indicated that numerous student services (academic advising, career counseling, skill labs, and tutoring) were highly important to students. Community college educators should consider the concept of cross programming in which several student and academic support services are bundled programmatically in a residence hall. This approach addresses the barrier of inconvenience, as numerous services are available to students concurrently.

During a registration blitz, a practical example of cross programming, representatives from numerous campus offices go to the residence hall during the registration period to assist students with all aspects of the registration process (R. Figura, personal communication, April 17, 2013). Based on CCCSE (2010a) data, the case can be made for staff from academic advising, career counseling, tutoring services, and various skill labs to come together for an evening program in the residence halls. Ideally, residence life staff would initiate this program, inviting staff from campus offices, setting up meeting space, and rallying students to attend. Essentially, this is an example of one-stop shopping where several student services are placed in students' paths. Since each campus is as unique as students' needs, the institutional context must be taken into account when designing programs to best support students.

Budgeting issues for student support services. As budgets are continually stressed, it is important to think strategically about critical elements essential to ensure the operational and programmatic vitality of the residence halls. Stimpson (1994) warned, "Operating budgets must be adequate to provide the supplies, materials, honoraria, and audiovisual support for program success" (p. 65). Still, colleges should also explore ways to offer services that may not significantly affect the budget. Some examples of enhanced services that do not significantly influence budgets include

- ◆ a registration blitz in which campus support offices (academic advising, career counseling, tutoring services, and representatives from various skill labs) meet students in the residence halls to assist with registration for the upcoming semester;
- ◆ academic advising in a residence hall, an approach that may not require an additional academic adviser, only a temporary relocation of the adviser to the residence hall for increased visibility and student access; and
- ◆ peer tutoring services that incorporate academic support into a residence life program by using students as peer tutors with oversight from a professional staff member. Paying peer tutors would be a minimal addition to a budget as well as an opportunity to provide on-campus employment for students.

Designing spaces that integrate student support. Similar to the previous discussion regarding classroom spaces in housing units, community colleges that are developing, renovating, or expanding their residence life programs have an opportunity to design spaces specifically for student and academic support services inside the residential facility. Strategically placing services in the residence is one way institutions can combat a lack of awareness of resources, as noted earlier. For existing residential facilities, educators may consider redesigning or adjusting space allocations in the residential facility to create a student services office on the main floor in a high-traffic area.

Ideally, the office area would include space where students could meet privately with staff.

Reconceptualizing the residential facility is essential when addressing the unique needs of the community college student population. The traditional model of two students in a room with a community bathroom down the hall does not meet the needs of the current student population, which is a much more diverse group of students. Four-year institutions are also moving away from the traditional notion of residence halls as simply places for students to sleep, offering an increasing array of living options and amenities (Abramson, 2010). Demographic data for family residences and related standard-of-living indicators reveal that increasing numbers of American children grow up having their own private rooms and bathrooms. Consequently, requiring students to live in a common bedroom can be potentially stressful to the students and present some challenges to the college. Ideally, institutions should plan on multiple room types (e.g., private, semiprivate) to address the variety of home living arrangements students are accustomed to. Considerations must also be made for students with spouses or children. Of course, college administrators must ensure that students with private on-campus living arrangements do not become isolated—all the more reason to provide on-site student support.

Providing gender-neutral floors in residence life. According to the Transgender Law and Policy Institute (2013), 97 colleges and universities provided gender-inclusive housing. Currently no two-year colleges are on this list; all 97 institutions listed by the institute are four-year institutions. A gender-neutral floor design is most often used in instances when traditional, same-sex room assignments are not suitable or fitting. This residential design allows for "housing in which students can have a roommate of any gender" (Transgender Law and Policy Institute, 2013, p. 1), which could include same gender, opposite gender, or other gender identities or expression to live together regardless of biological sex. The diversity of today's residential student suggests there should be intentionality in designing residential services to meet students' current and evolving needs as well as to provide a supportive residential environment. A gender-inclusive floor, as a residential design, is a programmatic option that administrators at two-year institutions may want to consider with respect to relevant demand data and particularly with respect to regional and cultural norms. Gender-neutral (also called gender-inclusive) floors in residence life, as well as theme housing such as a lesbian, gay, bisexual, transgender (LGBT) floor, are examples of residential programmatic options designed to provide a safe space for LGBT students and allies. Offering such options is a way that residence life staff can work to create a welcome and inclusive environment and ultimately a safe space for students, regardless of gender identity, expression, or sexual orientation.

Expand Professional Development Focused on Engaging Students

The third strategy in *The Heart of Student Success* (CCCSE, 2010b) focused on the need for professional development for faculty, providing opportunities to learn "more about effective teaching strategies and to apply those strategies in their day-to-day work" (p. 16). Just as faculty need ongoing professional development opportunities, so do individuals working in student services. Making an investment in staff through professional development can directly benefit students. Intentionality in developing a professional development plan for housing staff members is critical. If the ultimate goal is for staff to learn promising practices tied to student success, then these practices should be at the forefront of the discussion on selecting professional development opportunities. More specifically, "Leadership development interventions should be varied; possibilities include short-term education in special workshops, orientation sessions, forums on campus issues and broader social issues, skill-building sessions, and longer term development through leadership classes and community service commitments" (Komives, 1994, p. 232). Such training can also address the practical realities of leading student housing, including education with respect to safety and security, alcohol and drug use, student depression, violence, sexual activity, and social matters. Making staff training a budget priority, given increasing student complexities and legal realities, is critical to the success of a residential program.

To assist with the professional development of housing staff, organizations such as the Association of College and University Housing Officers– International (ACUHO-I) provide education and communication linkages for residence life professional staff. International, national, and regional conferences provide housing professionals with the opportunity to share best practices and to network. In addition to formal organizations, housing and residence life staff can turn to professional literature as they develop services to support community college students. Suggested resources include

◆ *Learning and Development Outcomes* (Council for the Advancement of Standards, 2008)

- *Standards and Ethical Principles for College and University Housing Professionals* (ACUHO-I, 2013)
- *Professional Competency Areas for Student Affairs Practitioners* (ACPA–College Student Educators International & NASPA Student Affairs Administrators in Higher Education, 2010)
- *The Journal of College and University Student Housing*

Additional examples of professional development opportunities include becoming a member of a professional association, attending a conference, participating in a virtual webinar with other student affairs professionals, visiting another campus to discuss approaches used to support students, or simply reading a book on best practices. Many professional organizations (including ACUHO-I, ACPA, and NASPA) have regional or state-level professional development opportunities that are less costly to attend than national or international conferences and serve to build local professional networks that may be especially helpful to community college leaders working with a new residential program. Most states have an association with affiliate groups, such as student services officers or housing officers, that also provide professional development opportunities at a lower cost and with a regional element. Finally, a variety of online supports include www.ResLifePro.com, www.residentassistant.com, www.studentaffairs.com, and other individual institutions' online resources. Regardless of the format, professional development opportunities for staff should be intentional, high priority, and ongoing.

Create Policy Conditions to Promote Learning and Completion

The final strategy recommendation in *The Heart of Student Success* is to create policy conditions to promote learning and completion (CCCSE, 2010a, 2010b). Specifically, the report encourages policies that create greater structure and fewer options for students, with the intention of increasing student retention and graduation.

Following this recommendation, administrators should review residence life and student housing policies to ensure that current policies promote learning and degree completion and that all policies are designed to keep students on track. Examples of such policies include requirements for students to be enrolled full-time, to make satisfactory academic progress, and to be current with their financial obligations to the institution. In addition, the policies should address the consequences of policy violations, such as placing the student on probation or requiring student services interventions. Policy conditions for housing and residence life programs should also include specific community college campus populations. For example, additional policies may need to be designed for specialized housing intended to accommodate students with children (Cohen & Brawer, 2008) or international students. If residence life programs provide access to on-site services such as tutors in residence, residential computer consultants, and writing centers in the halls to aid in degree completion, an accompanying requirement could be a minimum grade point average for a student to remain in on-campus housing.

A data-informed approach for actual practice is a way for housing professionals to be deliberate in their efforts to develop and refine on-campus housing programs. *The Heart of Student Success* (CCCSE, 2010a) advised,

> Build a culture of evidence. Good education is driven by passion, but it must be firmly rooted in evidence . . . [a culture of evidence] in which administrators, faculty, and staff use data to set goals, monitor progress, and improve practice. Individuals in a culture of evidence embrace data and share it widely because they know transparency builds credibility, ownership, and support for change. (2010a, p. 6; 2010a, p. 20)

Using national benchmarking data on community college student engagement augmented with institutional data is a suggested starting point. Often, national data such as the CCCSE (2010a, 2010b) are discussed at professional conferences; attending a professional conference and learning about current trends can jump-start institutional efforts to build a culture of evidence. It is important to note that if residential-specific data on community colleges are not available for analysis, there are ways to analyze broader data using a residential lens.

It is advisable to use quantitative data such as national and institutional statistics as one piece of the puzzle but not overlook opportunities for qualitative assessment. Residential staff members working with on-campus residents have direct contact with students and often insightful information regarding the needs of the residential population. A culture of evidence is a balance between empirical data (quantitative and qualitative) and insight from frontline residential and student services staff; together this information can aid in developing and refining residential programs that contribute to community college student success. At Jackson College, for example, the institution employs an institutional effectiveness and quality improvement approach, deploying a balanced scorecard on key indicators of success in student housing. Additionally, data are matched against other community colleges with housing programs to assist in establishing goals and performance measures. The overall performance of the college's student housing program is included in an annual report to the institution's board of trustees.

CONCLUSION

The CCCSE's (2010a, 2010b) *The Heart of Student Success* provides four strategies to support students' academic pursuits at two-year institutions, and this chapter expands the narrative to investigate ways residential programs can further support students' learning. The addition of residence life programs can reconceptualize the way one thinks about the community college experience. Residential programs can be an integral aspect of the student success puzzle and promote student retention and completion (Creamer, 1994). Still, simply providing a building for students to live in is insufficient to ensure a vital, sustainable, and successful experience for students. Developing a successful residence life program demands that intentional services to promote student engagement be designed and provided. Cohen and Brawer (2008) found the more that students used services, the more successful the students were. Data like these should motivate community college administrators to interweave student support services into the residential experience and enthusiastically encourage students to use the services. Such a model supports the academic mission of the institution and leverages the power of the residential experience.

Conducting a regular needs assessment is a step that community college leaders can take to understand the diversity of their students and their specific residential needs. A needs assessment focused on residential students can provide valuable insight regarding elements needed on campus to promote student success. Designing programs to address the particular needs of diverse students requires providing intentional support structures necessary for students to graduate. Program design as well as residential facility design can be significant in addressing students' academic needs. Ongoing assessment can inform practice in the early stages of planning facility construction, developing staffing and programming plans, and addressing evolving students' expectations from a housing experience.

The old adage "It takes a village to raise a child" has parallels on a college campus. This saying could be translated to the collegiate context as "It takes the college community to support students as they navigate the collegiate process." This knowledge suggests that a residential program is just one piece of the puzzle. There must be support from campus offices to collaborate on programs (Williams, 2002) and meet students where they are (in residence halls) to make residential programs viable. If campus partners are not invested, or collaboration is not valued at the institution, there is little reason to build residence halls aside from proximity to campus services.

One of the substantive advantages accompanying a residential program on a community college campus is the amount of time students spend on the campus. Improved student engagement ultimately adds to their satisfaction and leads to completion. Indeed, the college benefits from increased student involvement and participation in the college environment. Faculty and staff will have additional opportunities to interact with students and promote student learning and success, and these opportunities must not be squandered (Williams, 2002). Indeed, the creation of a residency program on a community college campus will change its culture. It is essential that campus leaders and boards of trustees thoughtfully consider all aspects of undertaking a housing program before implementation and obtain acceptance from the campus community as well as from the broader community it serves. Student housing has many benefits as well as attendant challenges. Without considering and embracing both of these elements fully, the community college may not achieve the overall success its administrators intended.

REFERENCES

Abramson, P. (2010). *Green and growing: Sustainability and amenities are increasing in new residence hall projects.* Retrieved from http://www.peterli.com/cpm/pdfs/2010-College-Housing-Report.pdf

ACPA–College Student Educators International & NASPA Student Affairs Administrators in Higher Education. (2010). *Professional competency areas for student affairs practitioners.* Retrieved from http://www.naspa.org/images/uploads/main/Professional_Competencies.pdf

ACUHO-I. (2013). *Standards and ethical principles for college and university housing professionals.* Retrieved from http://www.acuho-i.org/Portals/0/doc/res/acuhoi-standards-2013.pdf

American Association of Community Colleges. (2013). *2013 community college fast facts*. Retrieved from http://www.aacc.nche.edu/AboutCC/Documents/FactSheet2013.pdf

Bers, T. H., & Calhoun, H. D. (2002). Literature on community colleges: An overview. *New Directions for Community Colleges*, (117), 5–12.

Braxton, J. M., & McClendon, S. A. (2001–2002). The fostering of social integration through institutional practice. *Journal of College Student Retention, 3*(1), 57–71.

Brower, A. M., & Inkelas, K. K. (2010). Living-learning programs: One high-impact educational practice we now know a lot about. *Liberal Education, 96*(2), 36–43.

Center for Community College Student Engagement. (2010a). *The heart of student success*. Retrieved from http://www.ccsse.org/publications/national_report_2010/36379tw/CCCSE_2010_national_report.pdf

Center for Community College Student Engagement. (2010b). *The heart of student success: Executive summary*. Retrieved from http://www.cccompletioncorps.org/ccccorps/sites/default/files/pdfs/CCCSE_2010_exec_sum.pdf

Cohen, A. M., & Brawer, F. B. (2008). *The American community college* (5th ed.). San Francisco, CA: Jossey-Bass.

Council for the Advancement of Standards. (2008). *Learning and development outcomes*. Retrieved from http://www.cas.edu/wp-content/uploads/2010/12/Learning-and-Developmental-Outcomes-2009.pdf

Creamer, D. G. (1994). Synthesis of literature related to historical and current functions of student services. In G. A. Baker, III (Ed.), *A handbook on the community college in America* (pp. 309–318). Westport, CT: Greenwood.

Johnson, J. (2013, June 13). Massachusetts paves the way for community colleges to open dorms. *Washington Post*. Retrieved from http://articles.washingtonpost.com/2013-06-19/local/40058641_1_community-colleges-traditional-colleges-housing-options

Komives, S. R. (1994). Increasing student involvement through civic leadership education. In C. C. Schroeder, P. Mable, & Associates (Eds.), *Realizing the educational potential of college residence halls* (pp. 218–240). San Francisco, CA: Jossey-Bass.

Levinson, D. L. (2005). *Community colleges*. Santa Barbara, CA: ABC-CLIO.

Longerbeam, S. D., Inkelas, K. K., & Brower, A. M. (2007). Second-hand benefits: Student outcomes in residence halls with living-learning programs. *Journal of College and University Student Housing, 34*(2), 20–30.

National Survey of Student Engagement. (2014). *Annual results*. Retrieved from http://nsse.iub.edu/

Schroeder, C. C., Mable, P., & Associates. (1994). *Realizing the educational potential of residence halls*. San Francisco, CA: Jossey-Bass.

Stimpson, R. (1994). Creating a context for educational success. In C. C. Schroeder, P. Mable, & Associates (Eds.), *Realizing the educational potential of residence halls* (pp. 53–69). San Francisco, CA: Jossey-Bass.

Transgender Law and Policy Institute. (2013). *Colleges and universities that provide gender-inclusive housing*. Retrieved from http://www.transgenderlaw.org/college/index.htm#housing

Williams, T. E. (2002). Challenges in supporting student learning and success through student services. *New Directions for Community Colleges*, (117), 67–76.

Part Three

A Closer Look
Specialized Populations and Communities on Two-Year Campuses

THE FINAL SECTION OF THIS BOOK opens with a chapter on elder learners. Ramona Meraz Lewis, Eboni M. Zamani-Gallaher, and Christopher Bonapace underscore the rich history community colleges have engaging and welcoming diverse populations, particularly nontraditional adult learners. Shifting demographics illustrate a graying of society that is leading to what some are calling the growth of a third age learning community. Older adults have a wide variety of needs and interests in learning, including training for encore careers, skill development, making meaning, and leisure, and are among the increasing number of people seeking opportunities for lifelong learning. This chapter discusses the demographic changes that have led to elder learners enrolling in community college settings. More specifically, the contributors explore the motivating factors for college attendance during one's third age, integrate relevant theories of older adult learning, and highlight select programs that are exemplars for meeting the needs of older adult learners on two-year campuses.

An important subpopulation of students on community college campuses are veterans. Tara Fagan and Shaftone Dunklin explore readjustment and combat-related issues with veterans of Operation Enduring Freedom, Operation Iraqi Freedom, and Operation New Dawn.

More specifically, the authors review the demographics of this population, their prevalent mental health concerns, and physical injuries related to combat service. Fagan and Dunklin argue that there is an urgent need to prepare student services professionals for working with those veterans who experience stress related to combat experience, associated post-traumatic stress disorder symptoms, substance abuse, and suicidal ideation. The chapter closes with a review of best practices for student veteran services in higher education.

Enrollment patterns reveal that a growing number of community college students are from racially or ethnically diverse backgrounds. The majority of these students are also women. While reviewing the grim transfer rate for students of color, one cannot help but ask how to make the transfer function stronger. One technique in other sectors of higher education to improve matriculation has been student involvement. Dimpal Jain's chapter is unique in our book—it is original research. We felt it contributed to our goal of connecting theory to practice. She examines the relationship between involvement and persistence for women of color in a community college. Her chapter explores whether leadership engagement assists or hinders female students of color in their readiness to transfer. Moreover, her chapter illustrates intersectionality between race and gender and their effect on student leadership engagement.

Over the course of their existence, American community colleges have been known by many names, such as junior colleges, city colleges, technical institutes, and even democracy's colleges. Jesse S. Watson and Elizabeth Cox Brand round out the text in the final chapter by examining the research on social and cultural capital among marginalized students at community colleges. Unfortunately, in the current environment negative stereotypes may abound, and nondominant groups may experience marginalization. Drawing from their collective research and using a meta-analysis on marginalized populations at community colleges, the authors apply the concepts of cultural and social capital to examine the community college campus climate for various student groups. The chapter also provides pragmatic recommendations that student affairs professionals and student leaders can assimilate and implement on their campuses.

9

Older Adult Lea ⌐ ¬
Community Colleges

A New Wave of Adult Learners

Ramona Meraz Lewis, Eboni M. Zamani-Gallaher,
and Christopher Bonapace

BOOMERS ON CAMPUS. THE CLASS GOES GRAY. SENIORS BACK TO SCHOOL. Once thought of as novelty and innovative marketing tools to entice lifelong learners to college campuses, headlines such as these are now becoming more of a reality as life expectancy increases. Described by McCarthy (2006) as an "aging boom" (p. 34), by 2050 over one quarter of a million people will be 85 years of age or older. These demographic shifts and other societal changes have led many older adults and retirees to rethink the postretirement life phase as they seek greater civic, educational, political, and social engagement (Wilson & Simson, 2006). Aging baby boomers, who are living longer, are healthier, and are more educated than previous generations, are expected to demand greater educational and leisure opportunities, and many researchers suggest they will be seeking these opportunities on college campuses (American Association of Community Colleges [AACC], 2009, 2010; American Council on Education [ACE], 2007, 2008; Fisher & Wolf, 2000; Laslett, 1991; Manheimer, 2002; Wilson & Simson, 2006).

113

missions of education for the public good, communal involve-
open access, community colleges are uniquely positioned to
to this growing population of adult learners. The baby boomer sur-
conducted by Del Webb (2010), which was a follow-up to a 1996 study,
divided boomers into two segments: younger boomers turning 50 in 2010 (n
= 504) and older boomers turning 64 in 2010 (n = 510). More than half of
boomers indicated they are as active or more active than they were 15 years
ago, and nearly one third of the younger group reported undertaking educational pursuits, whether for employment, advancement, or personal growth.
Furthermore, older boomers reported that the best part about retirement
is the "freedom" and the most disappointing is "not being around people"
and "missing coworkers" (Del Webb, 2010, p. 47). Older adults across all
segments of society are indicating a desire to pursue learning and education
later in life for a wide range of reasons. The American Association of Retired
Persons (AARP, 2012b) member opinion survey (N = 135,000) found that
87% of members indicated one of their top concerns is "staying mentally
sharp," and 68% reported that "learning new things" is among their primary
interests (p. 10).

Concurrent with the graying (i.e., aging) of America is what demogra-
phers also refer to as a *browning* of society, both of which are occurring
in community colleges as 15% of students are nontraditional-age learners
(i.e., over 40 years old) and 40% of students enrolled are ethnic minorities
(AACC, 2013; Zamani, 2000). The data from the survey of baby boomers
indicate the desires of only one segment of older learners (Del Webb, 2010).
It is important to note that the marked differences in this cohort—race or
ethnicity, gender, educational attainment, and socioeconomic status—all
play a role in the way individuals view retirement. Socioeconomics, previous
educational levels, health, and race are all factors that either help or hinder an
individual from pursuing educational opportunities later in life (ACE, 2007,
2008; Wolf & Brady, 2010).

The growing population of older adults and the phenomenon among
senior citizens to embrace learning presents a unique programming opportunity for two-year institutions to cultivate new relationships with older
learners, particularly at a time when colleges are seeking innovative ways of
involving the community. Given that the first members of the baby boom
generation entered retirement in 2008, they will play an integral part in
shaping the retirement and learning trends of tomorrow. In 2011 baby
boomers ranged in age from 47 to 65. By 2030 all boomers are projected
to be over 65 years of age (Strauss & Howe, 1991). With the waves of baby

boomers retiring and interested in continuing education, two-year institutions are uniquely poised to be responsive to this often overlooked segment of the population. With the current resource deficiencies of many colleges because of the state of the economy, attention to older learners is not always purely altruistic; there are financial benefits to serving the needs and interests of the largest, most educated, and wealthiest cohort to date. Community colleges in particular can better position themselves to bolster enrollment and increase revenues by expanding their lifelong learning programs. There are opportunities for community colleges to expand not only the breadth but also the depth of offerings to include a more diverse group of older learners (ACE, 2007, 2008).

The topic of older adult learning is relatively understudied and ignored in comparison to adult learning in general (i.e., typically focused on students 25 to 50 years old). The growing interest in the promise and practice of older adult learning appears to stem from the graying of society coupled with the impact of the baby boomers. Because this demographic receives little attention in the community college education literature, this chapter focuses on older adult learning in the two-year context. For this chapter, we define *older adults* as those aged 50 years and older. This definition is based on recommendations from AACC (2009), which developed its Plus 50 Initiative to help community colleges that are focusing on the educational needs of those over the age of 50.

A BRIEF HISTORY OF OLDER ADULT LEARNING

Older adult learning, sometimes called elder learning, lifelong learning, or third age learning, is broadly defined and meets a variety of needs for older adults. Learning activities can be formal or informal and take place in a variety of venues, such as community centers, libraries, private agencies, hospitals, and colleges and universities. The *third age* terminology not only reflects the growing number of seniors who have increased longevity, health, and leisure time but also represents a philosophic change that has influenced the growth of older adult learning (Fischer, Blazey, & Lipman, 1992; Laslett, 1991; Manheimer, Snodgrass, & Moskow-McKenzie, 1995). The third age learning concept grows out of the four ages theory, a life course perspective dividing life into quartered segments. The third age, usually ushered in by retirement, began to be viewed as a time for personal enlightenment, self-actualization, and learning rather than as a time of decline or retreat.

The growth of the third age concept and older adult learning programs can be traced to more progressive theories that emerged about older adulthood. Those theories, in turn, influenced more positive societal views on older adulthood. For example, before the mid-1960s most of the research about aging considered growing old to be a problem. Older adults were seen as frail and in mental decline, and the theoretical models of the day emphasized disengagement. Hence, one theory of aging involves older people gradually withdrawing in a manner that produced a mutually agreed-upon separation between elders and society (Cumming, Dean, Newell, & McCaffrey, 1960). Theories of disengagement essentially promote the idea that retreat from society and decreases in social interaction are beneficial for older adults (Cumming & Henry, 1961). With this ideology prevalent, the burgeoning concept of older adults being open to learning, growth, and change was relatively unnoticed. These disengagement views only fueled the existing negative stereotypes about older individuals and Western society's cultural bias toward youth, still prevalent today, making it even more difficult for older adults to be seen as active learners. Fortunately, several positive movements during the 1960s and 1970s helped fuel interest in older adult learning. For example, the growing field of gerontology and new theories about aging, increasing activism against age discrimination, and the creation of policies and funding (e.g., the Older Americans Act of 1965 and Title I of the Higher Education Act of 1965 legislated funding to support continuing education divisions) promoted the growth of adult learning programs (Manheimer et al., 1995).

Lamdin and Fugate (1997) called the 1970s and 1980s the beginning of the graying of campuses. At the 1971 landmark White House Conference on Aging, policymakers declared education as a way to promote meaningful pathways to growing older. The underlying premise of the conference established education as a basic right; however, Congress did not go so far as to guarantee seniors access to educational programs but rather stated that people have the right to pursue education (Manheimer et al., 1995). The Conference on Aging highlighted the important role education could play in the lives of older adults, called for the expansion of older adult programs, and emphasized outreach to ethnic minorities, individuals from lower incomes, and those with poor health. Also at that meeting McClusky (1971) outlined five learning needs of older adults that he defined as coping, expression, contribution, influence, and transcendence (also cited in Fisher & Wolf, 2000; Hiemstra, 1998). The five learning needs presented a shift in thinking and helped pave the way for programs that fostered learning and development in older adults because they are built on the foundational belief in every individual's potential for learning regardless of age (Hiemstra, 1998). Because of the 1976 Lifelong Learning Act, state legislators began to enact bills that allowed individuals over 65 to enroll tuition free in colleges (Manheimer, 2002). However, since those initiatives were never fully funded by the government, colleges needed to find their own sources to support these tuition waiver programs. Today, many community colleges offer reduced or free tuition to senior citizens for auditing courses, but those initiatives are often underadvertised, underused, and underfunded at the state level. Community colleges were also among the first to develop offices and specific positions related to senior learning, and they were innovative in their response to senior learning needs by seeking grants and government funds to support programs for the aging (Manheimer, 1998, 2005). As we moved into the late 20th and early 21st centuries, we began to see a significant shift in the growth and development of older adult learning programs at community colleges. In a study conducted by AACC (2009), 84% of the 204 community colleges surveyed reported having some programs or services for older adults.

OLDER ADULT LEARNING AND BLENDED LIVES

The current climate appears to be ripe for enrolling elder learners. As people live longer and healthier lives, they want to continue engaging in meaningful activities. Older adults now approach their retirement years with expectations of staying busy intellectually, spiritually, and physically. The demographic, social, and technological changes in American society moved us toward a "blended life plan" (Cross, 1981, p. 12). Societal changes have essentially altered life trajectories and the timing of life events. There is now less distinction and more blending between education, work, life, and leisure pursuits. Just as patterns of formal education are less predictable today because of the social and economic impacts on society, so are the ways people approach retirement.

Settersten (2006) wrote about the concept of the changing "three box structure" (p. 5) of education, work, and leisure. Community college education is no longer bound by location, making the possibilities for formal and informal education more far reaching than ever before. Increased opportunities and higher aspirations for women and minorities, increased societal acceptance of career changes, and changing definitions of *retirement* and *leisure* all contribute to the growth of older adult learning across the three boxes (Cross, 1981; Jarvis, 2001; Jarvis & Griffin, 2003; Manheimer, 1998). These changing demographics provide an opportunity for community colleges to make their mark in responding to the needs of this demographic of older adults.

Older adults pursue education for a variety of reasons and take part in a diverse array of credit and noncredit offerings (AACC, 2010; ACE, 2007; Fisher & Wolf, 2000). While some are interested in personal enrichment or pursue learning for the joy of learning, others might be more focused on learning new skills or connecting with others. In this increasingly technologically advanced world, expressive and instrumental motivations for learning are becoming more intertwined in the lives of seniors. For example, a retiree may desire to learn a new technological skill such as the software GarageBand for sound editing primarily as a hobby, but he or she might also use the skill to develop a part-time career. Others may pursue education as a way of belonging; the ACE (2007, 2008) reports cited connectedness with others as one of the primary reasons elder learners pursue formal learning opportunities.

Vocational initiatives for the over-50 worker are examples of programs designed to address the need for learning for employment. An increasing number of older adults indicate the desire to work beyond the average retirement age. The U.S. Bureau of Labor Statistics (2008) projected that the number of workers aged 55 to 64 will increase between 2006 and 2016 by 36.5%; in addition, the population of workers aged 65 or greater is expected to rise by more than 80%. By 2016 workers in the 65 and higher age bracket are expected to account for 6.1% of the labor force, up 3.6% from their share of the labor force just 10 years earlier (U.S. Bureau of Labor and statistics, 2008). Because they are staying in the workforce longer, some seniors may find themselves in need of retooling their skill sets to keep pace with changing trends of the workplace. An AARP (2012a) member opinion survey reported that 50% of the 140,000 members surveyed indicated they were retired, yet 40% (two fifths) of them were still working. Some older adults may pursue second careers in retirement, often called *encore careers*, as a way to bring in a steady income, particularly given the economic crisis and the rising cost of medical care, insurance, and prescription drug coverage. The AARP (2012a) survey showed that 40% of members 50 and older were concerned about finding local jobs. However, not all older adults will need to continue to work for additional income; some desire to stay actively engaged, and others want to remain connected to their communities by providing service and volunteer work (AACC, 2009).

STUDENT DEVELOPMENT, OLDER ADULT LEARNERS, AND COMMUNITY COLLEGE PROGRAMMING

The benefits of learning are positively correlated with psychosocial, intellectual, and interpersonal gains. Research indicates that maintaining high cognitive function as well as staying engaged with life are important factors in helping older individuals retain satisfaction and physical well-being as they grow older (Bearon, 1996; Rowe & Kahn, 1998). Pursuit of education by older people has been shown to increase self-esteem, self-worth, and sense of quality of life and decrease feelings of isolation and loneliness (Orte, March, & Vives, 2007). The opportunity for social interaction and community building is as important as undertaking an educational activity (ACE, 2007).

Compared to general adult learning theories, there are fewer theoretical models that address the specific learning needs or the way learning happens for older adults. Many of the models that do exist have been outgrowths of adult learning theory (Fisher & Wolf, 2000). New and expanded models of older adult learning as well as educational programs need to reflect the broad diversity of thinking, feelings, personalities, and needs of older adults. Too often older adults are seen as a homogeneous group, when in fact with 50-plus years of varied life experiences affecting their personal growth and intellectual and emotional development, they are perhaps more diverse than any other age group (Fisher & Wolf, 2000; Jarvis, 2001). Age is a function of diversity, and older adults include a cross section of every segment of society—women, men, people of color, and those of various income, occupational, and educational levels. Thus, in serving the learning and development needs of older adults, community colleges that provide programming for older learners should take into account that the needs for seniors are as unique as the needs for younger learners. It seems that most programs in the past have offered a one-size-fits-all approach to older adult programs that ignores the diversity of thoughts, interests, and needs of older adults (Fisher & Wolf, 2000, p. 481). One example of this is the way senior programs tend to overemphasize leisure as the primary focus. Consider the number of cooking, knitting, and travel courses offered by colleges and communities. However, leisure is not the only interest of seniors. It is important to recognize the uniquely individual nature and diverse needs of the older learner and provide educational offerings that reflect various approaches and topics. Furthermore, educators need to see learning as a fundamental part of the life course across all ages and stages of life.

Further emphasizing the diversity of learning and development needs of older adults, Fisher and Wolf (2000) expanded the conversation on older adult learning by calling for educators to focus on the often "under-addressed" (p. 482) learning needs of older adults in the categories of learning for meaning making, learning for employment, and learning for inclusion. Learning for meaning making emphasizes expressive and transformational aspects of learning. Expressive needs are often understood as learning for learning's sake. But transformative learning goes beyond offerings of leisure pursuits, such as travel or foreign languages, and emphasizes learning activities that engage elders in self-reflection, particularly focusing on a dialogue that encourages meaning making and addresses the larger questions of self-actualization, identity, and purpose. Growth in this area is illustrated in the number of life review courses and programs focused on spiritual or critical transformation. The learning for employment category may be more instrumental, in that it often tends to focus on a more specific need such as learning a skill for a new job. Fundamentally, learning for employment for older adults is a new concept in that more and more older adults plan and desire to stay in the workforce; it transcends the stereotypes and earlier practices of pushing older workers out with the assumption they are incapable of learning new skills or technologies.

Finally, Fisher and Wolf (2000) contended that educational programs for older adults of the future must be critical and learner centered because this model challenges the negative myths that have prevailed about aging individuals for centuries—that they are in mental decline, over the hill, or past their prime—the very stereotypes that often hold back older adults from pursuing formalized learning. Critical models encourage learning experiences that empower older adults rather than limit them to leisure models of education. Furthermore, older individuals' self-sufficiency and remaining in control of their own lives are emphasized. Learner-centered approaches include involving instructional methods that are self-paced and making sure adults are intimately involved in the development of their own programs—hence the growth of learning in retirement communities. Most important, these learner-centered models are programs uniquely designed for, and often in partnership with, specific populations of older learners.

The categories of learning and development offered by Fisher and Wolf (2000) encourage educators to develop a rich array of programming opportunities for older adults that take account of the spectrum of difference. For example, they address the various social identities of the older adult as woman, man, parent, grandparent, partner, spouse, friend, employee, community member, and, most important, individuals who have the ability and perhaps the desire to be lifelong learners. Programs for the over-50 learner should be inclusive and take a multidimensional approach to include inter-generational learning as well as find ways to integrate those who have tradi-tionally been excluded from adult learning (i.e., seniors, minorities, the poor, and those with lower levels of education).

We note two glaring oversights in the research on older adult learning: the dearth of research that focuses on the experiences of diverse older learn-ers and the lack of literature regarding student development in community colleges across generations of learners. Thus, we encourage more disciplined inquiry on what is taking place in the two-year sector for older adult learn-ers. We ask higher education researchers to continue to expand their research to consider the learning needs of this rapidly growing subpopulation in the two- and four-year context.

SITUATING THE COMMUNITY COLLEGE CONTEXT

Community colleges have a rich history of serving the needs of the larger community and responding to the needs of diverse learners, particularly adult learners. Subsequently, it is not surprising that community colleges have been the postsecondary leaders in offering educational opportunities for older adults. Nearly 50% of older adults enrolled in credit-bearing courses at degree-granting institutions attend community colleges (ACE, 2008). Although it is obvious that seniors are participating in formal and informal educational programs, it is nearly impossible to get an accurate picture of exactly how many older adults there are because procedures for reporting age categories vary greatly by college, state, and agency. For example, some report older-age categories as 35 and older, while others report 50 and older. Furthermore, community colleges, the National Center for Education Sta-tistics, and the U.S. Census Bureau vary in how they define and track educa-tional participation, adult education, and lifelong learning. Despite the lack of uniformity, there is increasing interest in participation in a wide variety of educational and lifelong learning programs, and community colleges are leading the efforts in making these programs available (AACC, 2009, 2010; ACE, 2008).

Further evidence of growing interest in older adult learning are the reports released by ACE (2007, 2008) and by AACC (2009) that focus on the grow-ing population of older learners, call for higher education to respond, and provide practical suggestions for implementing older adult learning pro-grams and services on campus. The report by AACC provided a status report on the nationwide Plus 50 Initiative providing 15 community colleges with funding to support the growth of programs and services for older adults.

Although the topic is gaining attention and the numbers suggest a move in a positive direction, older adult programs, much like older adults in most of our American society, still tend to be undervalued, underappreciated, and somewhat invisible. Unfortunately, many of the programs that do exist often suffer from lack of support from institutional leaders and are underfunded or undermarketed, which is addressed later in this chapter.

COMMUNITY COLLEGE PROGRAMS FOR OLDER ADULT LEARNERS

Programmatic offerings at community colleges for the over-50 population generally fall into one of three broad areas of focus, the first and most popular of which is programs of enrichment, typically thought of as satisfying the over-50 student's desire for "learning for learning's sake" (AACC, 2009, p. 9). The second category, workforce training and career development, provides the over-50 population with the tools to upgrade their skills, reenter the workforce, or begin encore careers. The third area of focus is programs geared toward service and volunteering. These connect or match the over-50 population to various nonprofit organizations, schools, or faith-based groups and often support intergenerational connections with younger students either in the classroom or through service activities (AACC, 2009).

In addition to these three focus areas of programmatic offerings, many community colleges around the nation are also giving additional incentives to encourage the over-50 student to enter higher education. Several community colleges offer tuition discounts (up to 100%, or free tuition), specialized advising for older adults, and tailored courses or programs for the over-50 student. Although these are all positive endeavors, some inconsistencies and problems prevent over-50 programs from reaching their full potential, such as the following: minimum age requirements may vary for tuition discounts among institutions, free or reduced tuition may not apply to credit-bearing courses, and specialized advising may not be available at all locations. In addition, one of the growing issues is that some courses marketed to the over-50 student are not designed specifically with the older adult student in mind but rather are add-ons or outgrowths of programs for other populations. Sometimes the discrepancy in information, lack of visibility, and lack of uniformity among community colleges can cause confusion among potential students. To address some of these concerns, the AACC (2010) developed standards of excellence as a guide to support community colleges in developing their over-50 program offerings.

These standards, divided into the following categories, serve as a model of best practice and clearly outline the most essential factors to consider for community colleges adopting older adult learner programs:

- needs assessments and ongoing evaluation
- broad-based organizational and institutional support
- community partnerships
- learner-centered programming
- learner support services
- accessible and accommodating materials and environments
- professional development for faculty
- integrated and targeted marketing (AACC, 2010)

Rio Salado College in Arizona is one example of a college that meets many of AACC's standards for over-50 programs. Rio Salado College's program is marketed to over-50 adults interested in becoming certified as teachers. Rio Salado not only assessed the labor market landscape in Arizona to fulfill a need in the community; it also developed programs for the older adult student with or without a bachelor's degree. By starting with a community needs assessment and targeting marketing, the college has expanded access for the over-50 learner. Additionally, Rio Salado College has secured a $25,000 grant through the MetLife Foundation/Civic Ventures Community College Encore Career Initiative and created numerous partnerships in the community to make itself a viable institution for years to come. Institutions considering an over-50 program should examine Rio Salado College's (2009) program for additional information.

Cape Cod Community College in Massachusetts is another excellent example of how a college has built a learner-centered program to fit the needs of over-50 students. It was also a recipient of a $25,000 grant as a result of its goal to adapt existing programs to meet over-50 students' needs. Cape Cod Community College has a leading program because of its approach in tailoring learner support services such as advising, counseling, and career transition services for the over-50 population. The college is also unique in its delivery model because of its incorporation of peer mentors, small-group and individualized support, and skill development workshops led by peer tutors ("New Program to Discover Innovative Ways

Community Colleges Can Help Boomers Prepare for Second Careers With Purpose," 2007). It also has a widespread integrated and targeted marketing strategy.

The AACC standards offer a set of recommendations as a way of acknowledging institutions that currently provide exemplary programming for older adults, but they also provide a general set of guidelines for administrators hoping to develop programs on their campuses. In addition, these recommendations also provide ways to address some of the structural, demographic, and attitudinal barriers that keep older adults from pursuing lifelong learning opportunities.

BARRIERS TO PARTICIPATION IN OLDER ADULT LEARNING PROGRAMS

Despite the growing number of initiatives by community colleges to attract older adult learners, too few older adults are taking advantage of formal and informal opportunities for learning, and there is a lack of participation by diverse older learners. For all those enrolled in any adult or postsecondary adult education program, the largest participation rates are of White women reporting incomes over $75,000 (ACE, 2007). The benefits of learning and lifelong learning have been shown to have positive impacts across the life course; thus, it is unfortunate that not everyone has the opportunity to pursue opportunities for formal learning later in life (Wolf & Brady, 2010). There are several reasons older adults are not fully participating in elder learning programs; these barriers are classified by ACE (2007) as structural, demographic, and attitudinal. Low status, lack of institutional support, and lack of faculty investment are some of the institutional barriers. Many older adult programs are underadvertised (ACE, 2007; Bash, 2003; Manheimer, 2005). In our own review of websites and course offerings, we have found this to be the case; although some programs have an Internet presence, many do not.

Societal structural barriers also tend to widen the gap for people of color, people from lower socioeconomic backgrounds, those living in rural areas, and individuals with less education. Age, income, gender, and previous educational history have proven to be the most consistent predictors of older adults' participation in higher education (ACE, 2007). For numerous systemic reasons, people of color and the poor are often statistically less likely to pursue formal educational programs at the college and university level.

African Americans and Hispanics over the age of 55 hold fewer degrees in comparison to their White or Asian American peers (ACE, 2007; U.S. Census Bureau, 2012). Because previous educational levels are often the greatest predictor of pursuing formal learning activities in older adulthood, people of color who hold fewer degrees than their White peers are underrepresented in the older adult learning landscape. For those who did not previously attend college, the barriers may seem greater. Non-degree-holding elders may hear about and even be interested in pursuing on-campus learning options, but entering the unfamiliar terrain of the ivory tower may seem overwhelming or unwelcoming to them.

Socioeconomics also plays a huge part in why a larger percentage of older adults do not participate in college-based learning programs. Some colleges offer tuition waiver programs, but they often come with other conditions such as availability of space, permission of instructor, and additional course fees that might be out of the question for individuals on low or fixed incomes (ACE, 2008). Social inequalities accumulated over a lifetime are exacerbated with age because of individuals' lack of access and opportunities created by unfair social structures, embedded societal discriminatory policies, and inadequate governmental interventions (Angel & Angel, 2006; Hooyman & Kiyak, 2011).

Unfortunately, the divide between the haves and the have-nots continues to widen in old age. Finding ways to involve older adults in the elder learning landscape is an important step in closing that gap and provides opportunities for a greater number of individuals to benefit from the positive impacts of lifelong learning. Additional financial support and creative measures must be employed to expand opportunities for diverse elder learners. Finding ways to integrate underrepresented groups into the learning landscape will be one of community colleges' greatest challenges and rewards.

CONCLUSION

Community colleges continue to lead the movement in responding to the needs of a diverse citizenry, particularly in the case of older adults; yet, there is still work to be done. We encourage community college leaders to recognize age as a function of diversity and seek to foster inclusive campus climates for the diversity of learners, particularly older adult learners (Zamani-Gallaher, Green, Brown, & Stovall, 2009). Community college administrators and faculty can view this growing interest by a diverse group of older adults in taking part in college-based learning programs as an opportunity to integrate the older adult learner fully into the life and learning programs on their campuses. Hence, it is important to pay increased attention to those who have traditionally been excluded from the adult learning landscape, the diverse elder learner. Whether involving the community, alumni, or retirees, there are numerous opportunities and potential for growth of over-50 programs on the community college campus.

REFERENCES

American Association of Community Colleges. (2009). *Educating plus 50 learners: Opportunities for community colleges.* Retrieved from http://plus50.aacc.nche.edu/documents/Educating_Plus_50_Learners_Opportunities_for_Community_Colleges.pdf

American Association of Community Colleges. (2010). *The plus 50 initiative: Standards of excellence.* Retrieved from http://plus50.aacc.nche.edu/Documents/Standards_of_Excellence.pdf

American Association of Community Colleges. (2013). *Fast facts from our fact sheet.* Retrieved from http://www.aacc.nche.edu/AboutCC/Pages/fastfactsfactsheet.aspx

American Association of Retired Persons. (2012a). *AARP research & strategic analysis spotlight 2012 member opinion survey: Work.* Retrieved from http://www.aarp.org/content/dam/aarp/research/surveys_statistics/general/2012/2012-AARP-Member-Opinion-Survey-Issue-Spotlight-Work-AARP.pdf

American Association of Retired Persons. (2012b). *Findings from AARP's 2012 member opinion survey.* Retrieved from http://www.aarp.org/content/dam/aarp/research/surveys_statistics/general/2013/Findings-from-AARP-2012-Member-Opinion-Survey-AARP.pdf

American Council on Education. (2007). *Framing new terrain: Older adults and higher education.* Washington, DC: Author.

American Council on Education. (2008). *Reinvesting in the third age: Older adults and higher education: Mapping new directions: Higher education for older adults.* Washington, DC: Author.

Angel, R. J., & Angel, J. L. (2006). Diversity and aging in the United States. In R. H. Binstock & L. K. George (Eds.), *Handbook of aging and the social sciences* (6th ed., pp. 94–110). Burlington, MA: Academic Press.

Bash, L. (2003). Adult learners: Why they are important to the 21st century college or university. *The Journal of Continuing Higher Education, 51*(3), 18–26.

Bearon, L. B. (1996). Successful aging: What does the "good life" look like? *Concepts in Gerontology, 1*(3). Retrieved from http://www.ncsu.edu/ffci/publications/1996/v1-n3-1996-summer/successful-aging.php

Cross, K. P. (1981). *Adults as learners: Increasing participation and facilitating learning.* San Francisco, CA: Jossey-Bass.

Cumming, E., Dean, L. R., Newell, D. S., & McCaffrey, I. (1960). Disengagement: A tentative theory of aging. *Sociometry, 23*(1), 23–35.

Cumming, E., & Henry, W. E. (1961). *Growing old: The process of disengagement.* New York, NY: Basic Books.

Del Webb. (2010). *2010 Del Webb baby boomer survey.* Retrieved from http://dwboomersurvey.com/

Fischer, R. B., Blazey, M. L., & Lipman, H. T. (1992). *Students of the third age.* New York, NY: Macmillan.

Fisher, J. C., & Wolf, M. A. (2000). Older adult learning. In A. L. Wilson & E. R. Hayes (Eds.), *Handbook of adult and continuing education* (pp. 480–492). San Francisco, CA: Jossey-Bass.

Hiemstra, R. (1998). From whence have we come? The first twenty-five years of educational gerontology. *New Directions for Adult and Continuing Education, (77),* 5–14.

Higher Education Act, Pub. L. No. 89-329 (1965). Retrieved from http://www.house.gov/legcoun/Comps/HEA65_CMD.pdf

Hooyman, N. R., & Kiyak, H. A. (2011). *Social gerontology: A multidisciplinary perspective.* Boston, MA: Allyn & Bacon.

Jarvis, P. (2001). *Learning in later life: An introduction for educators and careers.* London, UK: Kogan Page.

Jarvis, P., & Griffin, C. (2003). *Adult and continuing education: Major themes in education.* London, UK: Routledge.

Lamdin, L. S., & Fugate, M. (1997). *Elderlearning: A new frontier in an aging society.* Phoenix, AZ: Oryx Press.

Laslett, P. (1991). *A fresh map of life: The emergence of the third age.* Cambridge, MA: Harvard University Press.

Manheimer, R. J. (1998). The promise and politics of older adult education. *Research on Aging, 20,* 391–414.

Manheimer, R. J. (2002). *Older adult education in the United States: Trends and predictions.* Asheville: North Carolina Center for Creative Retirement.

Manheimer, R. J. (2005). The older learner's journey to an ageless society: Lifelong learning on the brink of a crisis. *Journal of Transformative Education, 3*(3), 198–220.

Manheimer, R. J., Snodgrass, D. D., & Moskow-McKenzie, D. (1995). *Older adult education: A guide to research, programs, and policies.* Westport, CT: Greenwood.

McCarthy, P. (2006). *The seniors of today and tomorrow*. Retrieved from https://www. phonakpro.com/content/dam/phonak/b2b/Events/conference_proceedings/ adult_conference_chicago_2006/monday/2006proceedings_mccarthy.pdf

McClusky, H. Y. (1971). *Education: Background paper for 1971 White House conference on aging*. Washington, DC: White House Conference on Aging.

New program to discover innovative ways community colleges can help Boomers prepare for second careers with purpose. (2007). Retrieved from http://www. encore.org/new-program-discover

Older Americans Act, Pub. L. 89-73, 79 Stat. 218 (1965). http://www.aoa.gov/ AOA_programs/OAA/oaa_full.asp

Orte, C., March, M. X., & Vives, M. (2007). Social support, quality of life, and university programs for seniors. *Educational Gerontology, 33*(11), 995–1013.

Rio Salado College. (2009). *Rio Salado awarded grant to help retrain boomers for encore careers*. Retrieved from http://blog.riosalado.edu/2009/07/rio-salado-awarded-grant-to-help.html

Rowe, J., & Kahn, R. (1998). *Successful aging*. New York, NY: Pantheon.

Settersten, R. A. (2006). Aging and the life course. In R. H. Binstock & L. K. George (Eds.), *Handbook of aging and the social sciences* (pp. 3–16). Burlington, MA: Academic.

Strauss, W., & Howe, N. (1991). *Generations: The history of America's future, 1584 to 2069*. New York, NY: Morrow.

U.S. Bureau of Labor Statistics. (2008). *Older workers: BLS spotlight on statistics*. Retrieved from http://bls.gov/spotlight/2008/older_workers/

U.S. Census Bureau. (2012). *Table 229. Educational attainment by race and Hispanic origin: 1970–2010*. Retrieved from http://www.census.gov/compendia/ statab/2012/tables/12s0229.pdf

Wilson, L. B., & Simson, S. P. (2006). Civic engagement research, policy and practice priority areas: Future perspectives on the baby boomer generation. In L. B. Wilson & S. P. Simson (Eds.), *Civic engagement and the baby boomer generation: Research, policy, and practice perspectives* (pp. 247–266). Binghamton, NY: Haworth.

Wolf, M. A., & Brady, E. M. (2010). Adult and continuing education for an aging society. In C. E. Kasworm, A. D. Rose, & J. M. Ross-Gordon (Eds.), *Handbook of adult and continuing education* (pp. 369–378). Thousand Oaks, CA: Sage.

Zamani, E. M. (2000). Sources of information regarding effective retention strategies for students of color. *New Directions for Community Colleges*, (112), 95–104.

Zamani-Gallaher, E. M., Green, D. O., Brown, M. C., & Stovall, D. O. (2009). *The case for affirmative action on campus: Concepts of equity, considerations for practice*. Sterling, VA: Stylus.

10

Two- and Four-Year College Contexts for Student Veterans

Tara Fagan and Shaftone Dunklin

O VER 2.4 MILLION MILITARY SERVICE MEMBERS have been deployed to Iraq and Afghanistan in support of Operation Enduring Freedom (OEF), Operation Iraqi Freedom (OIF), and Operation New Dawn (OND), "with 37% having deployed at least twice" (Litz & Schlenger, 2009, p. 1).

> Furthermore, the demographics of the fighting forces have changed, with a high proportion of National Guard and Reserve troops serving in roles that many did not anticipate when joining the military. These individuals are older than their active duty counterparts, with established careers and families. Female service members, represented in higher numbers than ever before, have a high amount of exposure to direct combat and life-threatening situations. (Schnurr, Lunney, Bovin, & Marx, 2009, p. 727)

These veterans and their families encounter numerous challenges as they return home. Many deal with critical issues including mental health problems, physical injuries, and a complicated veterans administration system. Multiple deployments; combat exposure; and reservist, National Guard, or regular active duty status all can affect this population's ability to readjust to civilian life after the fast-paced, violent war zone.

Upon their return, many veterans begin or continue their pursuit of a college education. Almost half of student veterans in college are enrolled at two-year or community colleges (U.S. Department of Veterans Affairs [DVA], 2012b). As the number of veterans on college campuses grows, faculty, administrators, and staff must recognize that adjustment to college life is as difficult as adjustment to civilian life for these men and women. Understanding the unique needs and demographics of student veterans is the first step in supporting their success in college.

Given the number of veterans enrolled in community colleges, it is critical for administrators to gain an understanding of their student veteran population. According to the National Survey of Student Engagement's (2010) annual report, student veterans did not engage with the university or view their educational experience in the same way as nonveteran students. The data also suggest that first-year combat veterans feel there is little campus support for veterans, even at a time when most institutions are trying to increase the level of services they provide for this group.

The military status, age, and gender of the current population of veterans are different from those of previous conflicts. Active duty military personnel are contracted full-time and are typically stationed at a military base or near one. National Guard soldiers and reservists serve the military on a part-time basis. The U.S. Department of Defense (DOD, 2007) noted that in 2007 more than 50% of OEF/OIF veterans were in the National Guard or were reservists. The largest group of women veterans today served in the OEF/OIF operations, and in 2008 women made up 11% of OEF/OIF veterans. According to a DOD 2007 report on social representation in the U.S. military services, about 60% of military personnel is White, 22% Black, 11% Hispanic, and 7% other. The report highlighted that 40% of military forces are minorities, and African Americans are disproportionately represented in the military compared to the civilian population.

Since 2001 over 182,000 women have been deployed and about 50% of female OIF/OEF veterans reported using their educational benefits. Baechtold and De Sawal (2009) emphasized the necessity to address the needs of female veterans on campus, which may differ from male veterans'. Not only do female veterans have to deal with the residuals of war, but 23% to 30% of female veterans reported military sexual trauma while on active duty, and may need additional services. "Military sexual trauma (MST) is the term that the Department of Veterans Affairs uses to refer to sexual assault or repeated, threatening sexual harassment that occurred while the Veteran was in the military" (DVA, 2012a, para. 1).

Occupations of veterans vary, and educational levels range from high school diplomas to postgraduate degrees. The high proportion of reservist and National Guard representation also contributes to a wide variety of ages (18 to over 60), educational background, and vocational training. These new veterans are professionals, teachers, police officers, skilled laborers, entry-level employees, and full-time students. Increased substance abuse, mental health issues, physical challenges, and homelessness in this population are examined throughout this chapter.

MILITARY STRESS

Stressors vary in the combat zone, but regardless of assignment, exposure to this explosive environment is taking a toll on OEF/OIF/OND veterans.

> Troops are seeing more-frequent deployments, of greater lengths, with shorter rest periods in between—factors thought to create a more stressful environment for service members. The day-to-day activities of troops in combat vary widely, but some common stressors in the current conflicts have been identified as roadside bombs, IEDs [improvised explosive devices], suicide bombers, the handling of human remains, killing an enemy, seeing fellow soldiers and friends dead or injured, and the helplessness of not being able to stop violent situations. (Tanielian & Jaycox, 2008, p. 6)

According to the National Center for PTSD, a survey of OEF/OIF veterans concluded that 92% have known someone seriously injured or killed, 74% have seen a dead or seriously injured American, 47% have handled or uncovered human remains, and 33% have been responsible for the death of an enemy combatant or civilian (DVA, 2010a). Other stressors include military sexual trauma in the combat zone perpetrated by either military personnel or civilians.

Health consequences of these extensive and ongoing wars will continue to develop in veterans over time. The most common illnesses and ailments include musculoskeletal problems that are primarily joint and back disorders. Heavy body armor and gear weighing up to 75 pounds are possible culprits. Common mental health diagnoses include adjustment disorders and post-traumatic stress disorder (PTSD).

> Due to improved body armor and battlefield medicine, many troops are surviving injuries that in the past may have been fatal. These soldiers, however, are returning home with complex, multiple injuries. These "polytrauma" cases

often include brain and spinal cord injuries, vision and hearing loss, nerve damage, burns, amputations, musculoskeletal injuries, infections, and emotional adjustment problems. (DVA Research and Development, 2006, para. 1)

Early studies indicated that "10–18% of combat troops serving in OEF/OIF have probable PTSD following deployment, and the prevalence does not diminish over time" (Litz & Schlenger, 2009, p. 3). National Guard personnel and reservists may be especially at risk for PTSD (Litz & Schlenger, 2009). Multiple deployments, exposure to harsh environmental conditions, and operational stressors may result in a combination of mental and physical health problems.

Physical injuries associated with combat and military service may include spinal cord injuries, vision and hearing loss, nerve damage, burns, loss of limbs, and musculoskeletal injuries, to name a few. Back, knee, and joint pain are common issues as well. Further research needs to be conducted on the health effects of exposure to burn pits and other hazards, such as bullets made with depleted uranium and toxic embedded fragments from IED attacks. Long-term physical effects of exposure to various situations in the Iraq and Afghanistan conflicts remain to be seen.

SIGNATURE WOUNDS OF WAR: PTSD AND TRAUMATIC BRAIN INJURY

PTSD and related disorders are growing problems in the OEF/OIF/OND veteran population. A basic understanding of PTSD is necessary to appreciate the impact it has on the individuals who suffer from it. PTSD can occur after someone goes through a traumatic event like combat, assault, or disaster. It can cause significant distress or impairment in social, occupational, or other important areas of functioning (American Psychiatric Association, 2000). Symptoms of PTSD are often grouped into three clusters:

Reliving the event: Symptoms in this cluster include intrusive thoughts and flashbacks about the event as well as dreams/nightmares about the event and distress (both physical and psychological) when reminded of the event.
Avoidance/Numbing: Avoiding people and places that remind you of a trauma, as well as distancing from others and emotions are examples of symptoms in this cluster.
Hyper-arousal: Feeling keyed up, irritable or angry, and constantly on guard are common symptoms in this cluster. Difficulty concentrating and

falling/staying asleep can also reflect hyper-arousal. (DVA, 2012b, para. 9;
emphasis in original)

The evidence suggests that PTSD in this population is higher than in the
general population. According to the DVA (2012b), up to 30% of returning
veterans may develop PTSD. In contrast, 7% of U.S. civilians have PTSD in
their lifetimes. According to research following the early years of the current
conflicts in Afghanistan and Iraq, 11% to 20% of veterans developed PTSD,
a percentage that has risen over time.

Along with PTSD, traumatic brain injury is one of to the two combat-
related injuries referred to as the signature wounds of the Afghanistan and
Iraq conflicts (Tanielian & Jaycox, 2008):

> The Department of Defense and the Defense and Veteran's Brain Injury
> Center estimate that 22% of all combat casualties from these conflicts are
> brain injuries, compared to 12% of Vietnam related combat casualties. Sixty
> to eighty percent of soldiers who have other blast injuries may also have trau-
> matic brain injuries. (Summerall, 2010, p. 1)

According to the National Institute for Neurological Disorders and Stroke
(NINDS; 2010),

> traumatic brain injury (TBI), a form of acquired brain injury, occurs when
> a sudden trauma causes damage to the brain. TBI can result when the head
> suddenly and violently hits an object, or when an object pierces the skull and
> enters brain tissue. Symptoms of a TBI can be mild, moderate, or severe,
> depending on the extent of the damage to the brain. (para. 1)

PTSD in OEF/OIF combat veterans is often associated with co-occurring
disorders that include TBI, substance abuse, depression, and suicidal ideation
or intent (DVA, 2012b). As noted earlier, TBI is one of the signature injuries of these conflicts and requires a comprehensive examination. TBIs are
separated into three categories based on the nature of the injury. The mild,
moderate, and severe ratings are based on loss of consciousness, neurological deficits, and the Glasgow Coma Scale (NINDS, 2010). "Symptoms of
mild TBI include headache, confusion, lightheadedness, dizziness, blurred
vision or tired eyes, ringing in the ears, bad taste in the mouth, fatigue or
lethargy, a change in sleep patterns, behavioral or mood changes, and trouble

with memory, concentration, attention, or thinking" (NINDS, 2010, para. 1). "Moderate or severe TBI may have these same symptoms with a headache that gets worse or does not go away, repeated vomiting or nausea, convulsions or seizures, an inability to awaken from sleep, dilation of one or both pupils of the eyes, slurred speech, weakness or numbness in the extremities, loss of coordination, and increased confusion, restlessness, or agitation" (NINDS, 2010, para. 1).

PTSD with a comorbidity of TBI can cause significant impairment. The comorbidity of PTSD, history of mild TBI, chronic pain, and substance abuse is common and may complicate treatment and recovery from any single diagnosis (Summerall, 2010). Depression is a common disabling illness for those suffering from TBI. Major depressive disorder (MDD) is a mood disorder that interferes with an individual's everyday functioning. Individuals with MDD have a persistent constellation of symptoms, including depressed mood, inability to experience pleasure, or loss of interest in almost all activities, that occur almost every day for two weeks (American Psychiatric Association, 2000). Other symptoms can include significant weight loss or gain or a decrease in appetite; insomnia or hypersomnia; psychomotor agitation or retardation; fatigue or loss of energy; feelings of worthlessness or excessive or inappropriate guilt; diminished ability to think or concentrate or significant indecisiveness; and recurrent thoughts of death, suicidal ideation, or suicidal attempts or plans (American Psychiatric Association, 2000).

Evidence suggests that substance abuse often results from PTSD and often precedes depression (Tanielian & Jaycox, 2008). Since 2001 there have been major increases in the rates of suicide of active duty soldiers deployed in OIF and OEF (Jakupcak et al., 2009). PTSD is the most frequently diagnosed mental disorder among OEF/OIF veterans seeking DVA health care; therefore, suicide is a major concern (Jakupcak et al., 2009). "Suicidal ideation is associated with high levels of subjective distress in this population and serves as a crucial focus for treatment for a significant proportion of individuals with combat related PTSD" (Nye & Bell, 2007, p. 1144). "Some studies that point to PTSD as the cause of suicide suggest that high levels of intrusive memories can predict the relative risk of suicide" (Hudenko, Homaifar, & Wortzel, 2013, p. 1). An increase in suicide among this population is a major concern. "Controlling for age, MDD, alcohol abuse, and drug abuse, veterans with PTSD were over four times more likely to endorse suicidal ideation than those without PTSD" (Jakupcak et al., 2009). TBI, depression, and substance abuse often compound the sometimes devastating effects of this disorder.

READJUSTMENT AND REINTEGRATION

Readjustment and reintegration to civilian life can be difficult for veterans. They may experience financial difficulties, relationship issues, feelings of isolation, and feelings of being overwhelmed.

Physical reactions include having trouble sleeping, interrupted sleep, bad dreams, feeling jumpy, being easily startled, headaches, upset stomach, and increased substance abuse. Cognitive issues include problems with memory and concentration, avoiding talking about deployment, loss of trust, and lack of motivation. Experiencing flashbacks, avoidance of people or places, and work or school problems are common stress reactions. Emotional reactions include feeling overwhelmed, depression, irritability, feeling numb, frustration, guilt, trouble with intimacy, and feeling uncomfortable in crowded places. Behaviors that are lifesaving skills in combat are not acceptable behaviors in civilian life. For example,

> in combat: driving unpredictably, fast, using rapid lane changes and keeping other vehicles at a distance is designed to avoid improvised explosive devices and vehicle-born improvised explosive devices, [but] at home: aggressive driving and straddling the middle line leads to speeding tickets, accidents and fatalities. (Castro et al., 2005, p. 1)

More information on combat behaviors can be found in Castro et al. (2005).

Mental, physical, and emotional well-being will positively affect student veteran success and retention. Returning military service members should be encouraged to enroll with the local DVA's OEF/OIF/OND programs within five years of serving in the combat zone for free health care. All OEF/OIF/OND combat veterans are eligible to receive free enhanced health care benefits (with no copay) for any condition that may be related to combat service five years from the date of discharge. The DVA has made tremendous strides in caring for veterans, and the National Center for PTSD is recognized as a leader in conducting research and promoting appropriate treatment for veterans suffering from PTSD.

> The VA's polytrauma system of care has rapidly evolved to expand services for TBI among returning veterans as well. However, not all veterans receive their care through the VA. Over the past year, both DOD and the VA have come under congressional and public scrutiny regarding their capacity to address PTSD and TBI. Congress has directed billions of dollars to address perceived

capacity constraints, whether on human resources or financial resources; however, little is known to date about the capacity requirements for addressing the needs of the newest veteran population. (Tanielian & Jaycox, 2008, p. 8)

Education is the best way to prepare college professionals to support veterans in their adjustment to college and civilian life. A comprehensive understanding of the stress related to combat experience, associated PTSD symptoms, substance abuse, TBI, and suicide is essential. Remaining objective and impartial is equally important. Resiliency is the norm when service members are making the transition to civilian life. Providing good support to our service members is beneficial to the student veteran, the institution, and our society.

INDICATIONS FOR TWO-YEAR COLLEGES AND BEYOND

The Post-9/11 Veterans Educational Assistance Act of 2008, commonly referred to as the 21st Century GI Bill of Rights, significantly increased educational benefits for veterans serving on active duty after September 11, 2001. This bill is reflective of the 1944 GI Bill, as it provides eligible veterans payments for tuition, books, and housing. This new bill has helped pave the way for OEF/OIF/OND veterans to pursue higher education. Keith Wilson (2011), former director of DVA education, noted that in 2010 about 700,000 service members or veterans used educational benefits, 33% of whom were enrolled in community colleges. In 2009 the DVA reported that 5 of the top 15 schools that had over 1,000 veterans using Post-9/11 benefits were community colleges (Sewel, 2010). According to the DVA (2012b), "Most student veterans are enrolled in public two-year (43%) and 4-year institutions (21%). Almost an equal number of student veterans are enrolled in private not-for-profit schools (13%) and private for-profit schools (12%)" (para. 4).

California, Texas, Florida, and Virginia community college systems benefit from the active duty military bases housed in those states, as many service members take advantage of their tuition assistance while in the military. "Student veterans consistently report that the Post-9/11 GI Bill helped with their adjustment to school. Almost 25% of student Veterans report that the Post-9/11 bill was a major influence in their decision to pursue higher education" (DVA, 2012b, para. 2).

The Post-9/11 bill offers benefits for service members and veterans attending education and training programs at an accredited college or university.

According to the DVA (2013), the Post-9/11 bill provides financial support for education and housing to individuals with at least 90 days of aggregate service after September 11, 2001, or to individuals discharged with a service-connected disability after 30 days of service. Veterans must have received an honorable discharge to be eligible for the Post-9/11 bill. This benefit provides up to 36 months of education benefits, generally payable for 15 years following release from active duty. The bill also offers some service members the opportunity to transfer their benefits to dependents. In addition, benefits from the Montgomery GI Bill (1984) and various other educational support programs are available to veterans. The Montgomery GI Bill is sometimes referred to as Chapter 30 and provides educational benefits to individuals with at least two years of active service in the military. For more information, see DVA (2013), a valuable resource for student veterans and college professionals to remain current on the availability and eligibility of these financial programs that have a history of changing.

The National Association for College Admission Counseling (2010) reported that one third of college students transfer during their educational careers. Given the high number of veterans enrolled in community colleges, it is logical to believe that many will transfer to a four-year bachelor's degree–granting institution. Administrators must pay attention and address the needs of veterans whose intentions are to transfer to a four-year institution to assist them in making the appropriate academic decisions. Financial aid education can also assist veterans in making responsible financial decisions in seeking aid and paying for tuition. Veterans pursuing a bachelor's degree may want to consider exploring every option, including applying for federal financial aid and in-state veterans benefits or paying out of pocket for their community college education to preserve their entitlement for the most expensive part of their education, which would be at the university level. According to the American Association of Community Colleges (2013), tuition and fees for the 2012–2013 academic year in a public community college averaged $3,130, while the average tuition and fees for a four-year public institution were $8,660. When community colleges create good working relationships with veterans services staff working at four-year institutions, student veterans benefit.

Community colleges have a long history of educating college veterans and remain a prime choice for today's service members. Community college administrators are faced with many of the same issues four-year institutions encounter in addressing the needs of returning combat veterans and should study best practices of two- and four-year institutions alike. Community colleges can also continue to build on their relationships with local military installations because they provide a critical service: educating today's active duty service members.

BEST PRACTICES IN HIGHER EDUCATION

Institutions of higher education can be one of the leading providers of transitional services to help returning veterans readjust to civilian life. Each institution can help by providing training to staff to assist veterans in accessing their educational benefits, designating specific staff to assist student veterans with adjustment to college and civilian life, and creating opportunities for student networking among the student veteran population. In 2009 the Student Affairs Leadership Council identified four institutional models that categorize veteran services programs on college campuses, ranging from the one-person office to the comprehensive stand-alone resource center (Student Affairs Leadership Council, 2009). The most common veterans services delivery method is via the financial aid or registrar's office acting primarily in the role of certifying official, or the individual at the university who processes veterans' educational benefits (Student Affairs Leadership Council, 2009). To assist the growing student veteran population on campus, colleges should provide more services to veterans other than just processing their educational benefits. In 2007 the president of Camden County College in New Jersey changed how veterans received information from the financial aid office to a one-stop-shop veterans services center. The one-stop-shop model allows veterans to receive college services, academic advice, and financial aid assistance in a centralized place, a program that many colleges are now developing (Carr, 2009).

Administrators of institutions of higher education must remain mindful of the physical and psychological needs of returning combat veterans on campus. School officials can be prepared by having capable staff trained to deal with the complex issues veterans may have as they make the transition into the college classroom. The DVA (2010b) has also recognized the need for more veteran-directed services on college campuses, and that the DVA will do all it can to make sure veterans' experiences on college campuses are productive and fulfilling, specifically citing the role community colleges play in educating today's veteran.

Developed by the American Council on Education (ACE) and the Washington State Department of Veterans Affairs (WDVA, 2009a) *Veteran Best Practices in Higher Education* offers suggestions for those working with veterans. In addition, ACE developed best practices to improve services for veterans seeking higher education. "Colleges and universities across the country will need to seek creative solutions to improve outreach, access, and retention efforts to military veterans and remove unnecessary educational roadblocks to enhance their success" (ACE, 2008, p. 1). Suggestions from both documents include the following:

1. *Listen to veterans.* Hold a roundtable of high-level campus administrators and student veterans, or a veteran focus group. Establish some other activity where veterans can feel safe and supported to express their experience.
2. *Assess your institution's strengths and weaknesses.* Consider programs, services, and polices that could be initiated and improved.
3. *Start a student veterans group.* Start a veterans club or association.
4. *Design gathering spaces.* Offer a lounge area; space for advertising; and access to computers, printers, and tutors.
5. *Establish a point or points of contact.* Designate one person as the initial contact for veterans.
6. *Reorient student orientation.* Offer veterans an orientation about campus policy, legislation, and benefits updates; offer information about the veterans club and veterans resource team; and provide them with an opportunity to interact with peers, faculty, and staff to ease their transition.
7. *Build programs and access strengths.* This could be a local or community program. Student Veterans of America (www.studentveterans .org) provides ample online electronic resources for students and campuses.
8. *Educate faculty, staff, and students.* Provide comprehensive training that results in creating a supportive environment for veterans, staff, faculty, and administrators.
9. *Form partnerships with other organizations.* Colleges need the expertise and support of other sectors such as the DVA, Veterans of Foreign War, American Legion, Vet Center, Iraq and Afghanistan Veterans of America, and other agencies. Broad-based collaboration can ease the veteran from the military to school and from school to work.
10. *Involve the community.* Community members and alumni can take pride in an institution's program for veterans.

    Note: Families and dependents of veterans require assistance and support; remember to include them in the programs.

Free training and resources for college and university staff are available on the VA website (www.va.gov) (DVA, 2009a, 2009b).

Educating classroom faculty is an essential component of a campus with effective veterans services. Understanding the demographics of veteran populations and the impact of the military culture on student veterans is important. Creating an environment that fosters growth and reintegration for student veterans requires a commitment from administrative and academic leaders. An excellent resource for teaching faculty is the *Veteran Guidelines and Best Practices in the Classroom* (WDVA, 2009b).

CONCLUSION

Each institution is unique and can shape services for student veterans that match institutional resources and specific veteran demographics. Basic services can include a commitment to accurately prepare and verify federal and state educational benefits for student veterans. This includes remaining current with the ever-changing DVA benefit policies and procedures. Student veterans are typically highly motivated and seek productive and successful futures. Seamless and unambiguous access to quality education and student services that result in meaningful, productive careers is not a lot to ask for in return for military service. It is important to recognize the sacrifices made by military service members and ease their transition onto our college campuses.

REFERENCES

American Association of Community Colleges. (2013). *2013 community college fast facts.* Retrieved from http://www.aacc.nche.edu/AboutCC/Documents/FactSheet2013.pdf

American Council on Education. (2008). *Serving those who serve: Higher education and America's veterans.* Retrieved from http://www.acenet.edu/news-room/Documents/Serving-Those-Who-Serve-Making-Your-Institution-Veteran-Friendly.pdf

American Psychiatric Association. (2000). *Diagnostic and statistical manual of mental disorders* (4th ed.). Washington, DC: Author.

Baechtold, M., & De Sawal, D. M. (2009). Meeting the needs of women veterans. *New Directions for Student Services,* (126), 35–43.

Carr, C. (2009). Managing the enrollment boom. *Community College Journal, 80*(1), 22–25.

Castro, C. A., Hoge, C. W., Milliken, C. W., McGurk, D. Adler, A. B., Cox, A., & Bliese, P. D. (2005). *Battlemind training I: Transitioning from combat to home.* Rockville, MD: Walter Reed Army Institute of Research.

Hudenko, W., Homaifar, B., & Wortzel, H. (2013). *The relationship between PTSD and suicide.* Retrieved from http://www.ptsd.va.gov/professional/co-occurring/ptsd-suicide.asp

Jakupcak, M., Cook, J., Imel, Z., Fontana, A., Rosenheck, R., & McFall, M. (2009). Posttraumatic stress disorder as a risk factor for suicidal ideation in Iraq and Afghanistan war veterans. *Journal of Traumatic Stress, 22*(4), 303–306.

Litz, B., & Schlenger, W. (2009). PTSD in service members and new veterans of the Iraq and Afghanistan wars. *PTSD Research Quarterly, 20*(1), 1–3.

Montgomery GI Bill Act, Title 38, U.S. Code, §§ 3011, 3012, 3018A, and 3018B; and Public Law 110-252 (1984).

National Association for College Admission Counseling. (2010). *Special report on the transfer admission process.* Retrieved from http://www.nacacnet.org/research/research-data/Documents/TransferFactSheet.pdf

National Institute for Neurological Disorders and Stroke. (2010). *Traumatic brain injury.* Retrieved from http://www.ninds.nih.gov/disorders/tbi/tbi.htm

National Survey of Student Engagement. (2010). *NSSE 2010 Overview.* Bloomington, IN: Author.

Nye, E. C., & Bell, J. B. (2007). Specific symptoms predict suicidal ideation in Vietnam combat veterans with chronic post-traumatic stress disorder. *Military Medicine, 172*(11), 1144–1147.

Post-9/11 Veterans Educational Assistance Act, 38 U.S.C., Chapter 33 (2008).

Schnurr, P. P., Lunney, C. A., Bovin, M., & Marx, B. (2009). Posttraumatic stress disorder and quality of life: Extension of findings to veterans of the wars in Iraq and Afghanistan. *Clinical Psychology Review, 29*(8), 927–935. doi:10.1016/j.cpr.2009.08.006

Sewel, M. (2010, June 13). Veterans use new GI Bill at for-profit and 2-year colleges. *The Chronicle of Higher Education.* Retrieved from http://chronicle.com/article/Veterans-Use-Benefits-of-New/65914/?sid=at&utm_source=at&utm_medium=en

Student Affairs Leadership Council. (2009). *From military service to student life: Strategies for supporting student veterans on campus.* Washington, DC: Education Advisory Board.

Summerall, E. L. (2010) *Traumatic brain injury and PTSD.* Retrieved from http://www.ptsd.va.gov/professional/co-occurring/traumatic-brain-injury-ptsd.asp

Tanielian, T., & Jaycox, L. H. (2008). *Invisible wounds of war: Psychological and cognitive injuries, their consequences, and services to assist recovery.* Santa Monica, CA: RAND Center for Military Health Policy Research.

U.S. Department of Defense. (2007). *Population representation in the military.* Retrieved from http://prhome.defense.gov/portals/52/Documents/POPREP/poprep2007/download/ExecSum2007.pdf

U.S. Department of Veterans Affairs. (2010a). *PTSD: Center for PTSD. An overview of the mental health effects of serving in Afghanistan and Iraq.* Retrieved from http://www.ptsd.va.gov/public/PTSD-overview/reintegration/overview-mental-health-effects.asp

U.S. Department of Veteran Affairs. (2010b). *VA announces expansion of VetSuccess on campus pilots: New program eases veterans' transition to college life.* Retrieved from http://www.va.gov/opa/pressrel/pressrelease.cfm?id=1978

U.S. Department of Veterans Affairs. (2012a). *Military sexual trauma.* Retrieved from www.mentalhealth.va.gov/msthome.asp

U.S. Department of Veterans Affairs. (2012b). *What are common adjustment experiences? PTSD in student veterans.* Retrieved from http://www.mentalhealth.va.gov/studentveteran/adjustment.asp#five

U.S. Department of Veterans Affairs. (2013). *Post-9/11 GI Bill and other programs.* Retrieved from http://gibill.va.gov/benefits/index.html

U.S. Department of Veterans Affairs, Research and Development. (2006). *OIF/OEF: Operation Iraqi Freedom/Operation Enduring Freedom.* Retrieved from http://www.research.va.gov/resources/pubs/docs/oif-oef_fact_sheet.pdf

Washington State Department of Veterans Affairs. (2009a). *Veteran best practices in higher education: Ten ways to become more vet friendly.* Retrieved from http://www.dva.wa.gov/PDF%20files/Best%20Practices%20for%20Veterans%20in%20Higher%20Education%20_2_.pdf

Washington State Department of Veterans Affairs. (2009b). *Veteran guidelines and best practices in the classroom.* Retrieved from http://www.dva.wa.gov/PDF%20files/Veteran%20Best%20Practices%20in%20the%20Classroom%20.pdf

Wilson, K. (2011, June). *Veterans benefits administration business line overview.* Paper presented at the meeting of the National Association of Veteran Program Administrators, Cleveland, OH.

11

Women Community College Student Leaders of Color

An Examination of Student Involvement Theory

Dimpal Jain

TRANSFERRING TO FOUR-YEAR INSTITUTIONS for students of color has become a national crisis. For the past decade, the transfer rate has remained at 25% across America despite students' high aspirations to attain a baccalaureate degree (Wassmer, Moore, & Shulock, 2004). In addition, colleges with a higher percentage of either Latino or African American students have lower transfer rates even when controlling for academic preparation and socioeconomic status (Wassmer et al., 2004). While reviewing the grim transfer rate for students of color, one approach is to look toward other sectors of higher education for persistence strategies. A particular strategy that has gained widespread attention in four-year colleges or universities is to ensure that students become involved with campus life.

According to Astin (1984), an example of an involved student is one who "devotes considerable energy to studying, spends much time on campus, participates actively in student organizations, and interacts frequently with faculty members and other students" (p. 297). This definition of an *involved student* has been highly regarded in higher education literature (Rendón, Jalomo, & Nora, 2000) and has led to the widespread belief that participation in extracurricular student activities is a mechanism that ensures academic success (Abrahamowicz, 1988; Astin, 1984; Pascarella & Terenzini,

2005). The aim of this chapter is to explore involvement at the community college level and to examine the relationship between involvement and transfer for women-of-color student leaders.

This examination occurs at a critical junction in the educational pipeline: the transition from community college to a four-year college. The study presented in this chapter addressed the primary research question of how leadership experience assists or hinders a woman of color student's readiness to transfer. Transfer readiness applies to those students who are engaged in transfer-related course work and activities such as attending transfer workshops, applying for scholarships, and making counselor visits. Transfer readiness does not mean that a student has to be immediately applying to transfer; rather that he or she is in preparation to transfer at some point on his or her academic path.

The subsequent research question explores how race and gender affect these students' leadership engagement. In accordance with Bernal's (1998) definition of *leadership*, the term defined here goes beyond holding an elected or appointed position in a recognized organization. It also includes those who organize without titles, consider themselves activists, raise consciousness among members, and help plan and implement activities without formal recognition.

THE IMPORTANCE OF COMMUNITY COLLEGES

Community colleges are lauded as vehicles for social mobility and being "democracy's open door" (Connor & Griffith, 1994) to higher education because of their universal open-access policy (Brint & Karabel, 1989; Rhoads & Valadez, 1996). Community colleges fulfill multiple missions (Bailey & Morest, 2006), including the transfer function, which facilitates student transfer to four-year colleges or universities and the gateway to baccalaureate attainment. The ability and opportunity to transfer for students of color becomes salient in their pursuit of upward mobility. For "these are the very students that society expects to cross class boundaries, and a college-based education is the ticket to the top of the academic and social ladder" (Rendón, 1993, p. 7). Because community colleges serve nearly half or more than half of all students of color in the nation (American Association of Community Colleges [AACC], 2013), the academic and cocurricular opportunities for these populations are in many ways structured by the community college experience.

The most often cited theory when examining the relationship between involvement in extracurricular activities and academic success is Astin's (1984) theory of involvement. Although Astin's theory does not look at leadership per se, it is central in reexamining the relationship between involvement in out-of-class environments and persistence. Because transferring for students of color in community colleges is such a critical issue in the nation, it is worth examining student leadership to see what role, if any, it plays in terms of transfer preparation. Overall, research is lacking in the area of a student life culture on community college campuses and how leadership and involvement affect students' lives while they are attending this sector of higher education (Jain, 2009).

STUDENT LEADERSHIP

Although there is a paucity of community college student leadership literature, a few studies examine the roles of clubs and organizations. Friedlander, Murrell, and MacDougall (1993) developed the Community College Student Experiences Questionnaire, a survey that covers a variety of student engagement items. In addition, researchers at the University of Texas at Austin developed the Community College Survey of Student Engagement, a companion to the National Survey of Student Engagement for four-year institutions that also examines the role of student life on campus (Center for Community College Student Engagement, 2013). What these instruments fail to capture, however, are the nuanced differences within these colleges, namely the role of student leaders and the nuanced experiences of women and students of color.

Overall, little demographic information has been collected on student leaders and how their leadership might differ by race and gender while in community college. This is aligned philosophically with the fact that most student development and leadership models are based on a White male upper-middle-class orientation of power (Kezar & Moriarty, 2000). Therefore, the prevailing ideology of student leadership literature supports and maintains the ideals of those who are in positions of power: White upper-middle-class men. Research has been expanded to include women's and people of color's definitions of *leadership* only recently (Arminio et al., 2000; Chang, 2002; Harper & Quaye, 2007; Jain, 2009; Kezar & Moriarty, 2000).

STUDENT INVOLVEMENT THEORY

Astin's (1984, 1999) theory has its roots in a longitudinal study of four-year college dropouts conducted in 1975. He found that students who remained in college were involved, whereas those students who dropped out were not involved (Astin, 1984). In addition, he found that participation in extracurricular activities was significantly related to staying in college, and the type of college a student attends also affects his or her retention. Astin (1984) asserted that a "student's chances of dropping out are substantially greater at a 2-year college than at a 4-year college" (p. 100).

> Community colleges are places where the involvement of both faculty and students seems to be minimal. Most (if not all) students are commuters, and a large portion attend college on a part-time basis (thus, they presumably manifest less involvement simply because of their part-time status). (Astin, 1984, p. 100)

These findings supported his theory that student persistence was related to personal involvement in campus life.

Although the theory of student involvement has had a long-standing impact on the understanding of student persistence, other scholars have argued that Astin's (1984) original theory did not include the experiences of nontraditional students. Rendón and colleagues (2000) stated, "While the importance of involvement cannot be negated, these researchers [who have studied nontraditional students] note that many students, especially nontraditional students, find it difficult to get involved" (pp. 145–146).

Rendón and colleagues (2000) defined *traditional students* as those from upper- to middle-class backgrounds who are predominantly White, are from families in which at least one parent has attended college, and for whom the expectation of college attendance is well established. On the other hand, nontraditional students often come from working-class backgrounds, are older, work at least part-time, hail predominantly from communities of color, and are the first generation in their family to attend college. It is important to note that students in community colleges often come from nontraditional backgrounds: 40% identify as first generation, 16% as single parents, 7% as non-U.S. citizens, 3% as veterans, and 12% as students with disabilities (AACC, 2013).

Astin's (1984) theory also fails to answer the basic question of if and how student involvement can differ for students based on their race or gender. There appears to be no explanation for those students who may not persist despite their high levels of involvement and how they may experience their involvement in a specifically racialized and gendered way.

Although it has been well documented that involvement matters for college students, what has not been adequately documented is "*how* involvement is shaped within the context of differing institutions of higher education by student educational experiences" (Tinto, 1997, p. 600).

Astin (1984) did not account for students who are involved at community college campuses, namely student leaders, despite their part-time status. Rather, Astin's involvement theory paints community college students as monolithic and static, too busy to get involved in campus life.

CRITICAL RACE THEORY AND WOMANISM

To assist in a critical examination of student involvement theory, I turn to critical race theory (CRT) and womanism. According to CRT race is a social construct, and racism occurs implicitly and explicitly at micro (i.e., individual) and macro (i.e., institutional) levels (Solórzano, 1998). CRT in education is used to highlight the creation and maintenance of inequalities experienced by people of color (Ladson-Billings & Tate, 1995). Solórzano (1998) defined *CRT* in education as a theory that "challenges the dominant discourse on race and racism as they relate to education by examining how educational theory, policy, and practice are used to subordinate certain racial and ethnic groups" (p. 122). Although CRT centers on racial discourse, it also acknowledges its intersection with class, gender, and sexuality (Delgado & Stefancic, 2001).

Womanism allows me to explicitly and unapologetically explore the lives of women of color by centralizing race and gender in a simultaneous manner. Coined by Alice Walker (1983), *womanism* is broadly defined as an epistemological perspective based on the collective experiences of Black women or women of color that elevates all forms of oppression (Jain & Turner, 2012; Phillips, 2006). In this study, womanism and CRT are used to centralize the woman of color and acknowledge that the intersection between race and gender provides a specific outlook to her lived experience. This intersection is crucial to understand as it complicates traditional notions of involvement and transfer preparation.

COASTAL COMMUNITY COLLEGE PROFILE

This qualitative study included interviews and participant observation. Qualitative inquiry allowed me to develop a level of detail about my site and to be highly involved in the experiences of my participants (Creswell, 2002).

The study took place at Coastal Community College (CCC) in Coastal City, California (both pseudonyms). CCC is one of the prominent transfer institutions that sends students to the local top-tier research universities in the southern California area. CCC is one of 112 community colleges in California, which serve more than 2.6 million students, representing the largest system of higher education in the nation (California Community Colleges Chancellor's Office, 2013). In the spring of 2008, more than 30,000 students were enrolled in CCC; 60% were minority students and nearly 60% were women, with the average age of 25 years. It is estimated that nearly 1,000 students were involved in student activities and organizations.

I focused my attention on four racial ethnic student organizations for the duration of an academic year through participant observation. The four organizations (all pseudonyms) were United Latino Students (ULS), Black Student Union (BSU), Native American Students (NAS), and the Pilipino Student Union (PSU). These organizations were chosen to present a panethnic perspective on leadership and transfer. Through reputational sampling, three women were chosen from each organization (I was able to secure only two participants from NAS because of the severe underrepresentation of Native American students on campus) who hold formal or informal leadership positions, totaling 11 participants.

Each woman was interviewed twice over the course of an academic year at key transfer readiness points. In addition, a focus group interview was conducted, and my reflections were voice recorded immediately following the interviews. Validity issues were addressed through data triangulation and member checks (Maxwell, 1996). Each woman received a copy of her transcript, and we spoke about the initial interview and preliminary findings prior to her second interview.

Women-of-Color Student Leaders at CCC

The self-reported ethnicities of the 11 women who participated in this study over the course of an academic year were African American, Chicana, Dominican, Salvadoran American, Latina, Native American, and Pilipina. The age of my participants ranged from 18 to 34, with 20 being the average age. More than half the women were first-generation college students and worked as they attended school. These students also commuted long distances to CCC, rather than attending the community college near their home, largely because of the famed reputation of CCC.

Overall, these 11 women represented an accurate profile of local and national community college students (Provasnik & Planty, 2008): a single mother, an older returning student, an undocumented student, and full-time and part-time students. Most had family responsibilities at home, and their goals included transfer to a California State University campus, a University of California campus, a private local college, or an out-of-state college. In addition, all the women were a testament to the fact that it often takes students more than two years to transfer, illustrating that calling community colleges *two-year colleges* is a misnomer (Hagedorn, Moon, Cypers, Maxwell, & Lester, 2006). Only one woman, Paola, was applying to transfer during the course of this study; the rest applied in the following academic year or the next, a total time at CCC of three to four years. (Pseudonyms are used in place of the participants' real names.)

Academics and Leadership

Overall, I found that leadership positions for women leaders of color served as a support and a deterrent as they were preparing to transfer. Some students discussed how their experience as leaders was a large part of their academic success, while others described how their leadership was the sole reason for their academic decline. Christina, a second-generation college student with activist Pinoy parents, found her tenure as president of PSU extremely difficult, nearly resulting in a coup to oust her. Because of her tenuous term, she experienced a strained relationship between her academics and her leadership. When asked how her courses were going, she replied:

> Since I was really involved this semester not as well as I hoped it could be, but I mean I'm allowed to have a bad semester, so that's fine enough for me. So next semester I'm just going to take it slow and just try to focus on my academics, because I had my taste of a leadership position but now I just want to be able to get out of CCC.

Often we discuss how involvement or leadership can be seen as a panacea for academic success—in this case, transfer preparation—but here Christina demonstrated a more complex relationship. She states that because she was involved, she did not do as well as she would have hoped; this is a proclamation that goes against conventional involvement literature. She also stated that after experiencing a role in leadership, she wanted to be able to leave

CCC, suggesting that holding and maintaining a leadership position would preclude her from transferring from the school.

The same question was asked of Jackae, a returning student, single mother, and the director of activities for BSU:

> I find that the BSU club, and being a leader in that, being director of activities is just like that: it's up here [puts hands up high] but my classes are down here [puts hands down low]. Just because it's fun, all these people I have to please, and I'm good at it, I can do it. Classes, like English and math, I'm like, "Oh gosh, I don't know how to do this." So I'm trying really hard to stay in class, and finish them.

Here Jackae shared a sentiment that was common with the other women—at times academics became second to their club involvement because they found themselves better equipped at organizing for the club than mastering their academic material. In addition, they felt it was their responsibility as women to carry the club and to compensate for the other members' lack of commitment.

Keiana, who hoped to transfer to a historically Black college or university and was secretary of BSU, had this to say: "I do try to step up any way I can to help out, and if there's something I don't feel like doing, if I know it's for the group, I do it. And a lot of times, I do put things behind for the group. So the group is in the forefront."

In contrast, Paola, vice president of BSU, said that regardless of her club commitment, she felt that it was up to her to succeed and that CCC in particular helped facilitate her transfer preparation:

> I feel like I'm really prepared, I feel like it's a great school, I feel like this could be a university if they put their time into it, so I feel like I'm going to definitely be prepared. I think that a lot of how a student does depends on the student and themselves, so to me it's like I could have all the preparation I need from here and if I don't put forth my best effort it's not going to help.

An industrial engineering major, Paola felt that regardless of, or in addition to, her involvement in BSU, CCC has helped her feel academically prepared and ready to transfer.

Students overall brought up positive and negative aspects associated with their leadership roles. However, in the majority of the leadership literature, only the positive aspects receive attention. Some students struggled with their involvement, which had serious consequences for their academic success and transfer preparation. Two students failed their transferable math courses in the fall because of their leadership involvement and had to retake them in the spring, delaying their time to transfer for up to one year.

Race and Leadership

It is important to remember that these students were leaders in racial or ethnic organizations, and that organizing in this type of environment may be different in that their race is salient in all they do, as opposed to being in an organization that is centered on a particular belief or activity. Here race is being experienced in a myriad of ways: Not only were they made aware of their own race or ethnicity as they organized, but also the racial or ethnic nature of their organizing became prevalent. Carly, who identifies as Salvadoran American and commuted over two hours via public transportation to attend CCC, said she is active with NAS for the following reason:

> By me getting involved, I've been able to get into different stuff that I've never thought before, just on how America was founded and how we as Americans are in society. So that kind of gives you a different perspective toward how we "found" this country, and just who I am, and what my ethnic background is. By me being involved in that club, those questions [that] have arised [sic] in my head, I've completely ignored before that.

Here Carly demonstrated how NAS helped her arrive at a different consciousness about her own racial background and the racial background of America. One of the only three active officers in NAS, and one of the many Salvadorians in the club overall, Carly continued to say that the reason she was involved was because "I want to know more about the culture, and within knowing about more of its origins I can kind of understand myself and at the same time it stimulates my mind politically."

Similarly, in Jackae's discussion about her experience as a BSU member, she said: "It feels good to be around people that you know, and [with] people of your culture and race it's even better. And then they pump you up. And it's good, so that in itself has been really, really great." Here Jackae demonstrates how her own self-confidence increased and that she felt a sense of camaraderie by being in a club that focuses on African Americans.

Conversely, Jackae also revealed the weight of being a representative of a club like BSU. While discussing a major event at CCC called "Club Row" in which all registered student organizations have booths, sell items, and recruit new members for their clubs every semester, she had this to say:

> We gave people certain jobs and not everyone did it, so I kind of felt like it was my responsibility to just make sure everything was okay. Even though it wasn't because I'm not the president, but it's our club, we're representing Black people, our Black Student Union, and they're [students attending Club Row] going to be like, "What happened?"

Here Jackae felt that she had to compensate for the other club members' lack of commitment. She knew how BSU would be perceived if they appeared subpar to the other clubs participating in Club Row and was seriously concerned about how this reflected on Black people as a whole.

In listening to Jackae's and Carly's experiences we heard about issues related to racial and ethnic student organizations, topics that do not appear in a standard student engagement survey nor fit neatly into a question-and-answer format with check-off boxes for yes or no. It must be recognized that these students' raced work is unique (Rhoads, 1998), and can pose its own challenges and rewards in terms of leadership, and that their raced identities also intersect with their gender.

Gender and Leadership

For the women in this study, their gender, in addition to their race, often formed their leadership experiences. A common theme among these women was how their student organizations were often treated as dating sites and how this made them feel uncomfortable. Christina said that as president of PSU she created a partnership with another community college's Pilipino club and was a bit conflicted about her decision:

> They love our club and we love them, but I guess, again back to the social thing, because at PSA [the neighboring community college's Pilipino club] they have more guys and then CCC has more girls . . . so I guess for them even though we still do stuff together, it's still a social thing, like they come for our girls. But I don't know, it brought us together, so I mean it's good.

Here Christina had to admit that her alliance building with another regional community college came at the expense of socializing and dating opportunities for the men in the other Pilipino student club.

In addition, Paola and Keiana of BSU mentioned how the male president of their club treated elections as dating opportunities for himself. When referring to an informal officer appointment awarded to another BSU woman member, Paola stated,

> Everybody thinks [the BSU male president] put her [the other woman] there because she's cute, and we know that he's done it before, because he told me . . . because I didn't win any of the elections. I had run for president, I didn't win it. He told me, "Oh, I let you have ICC Rep [interclub council representative]" because of that too [being cute].

Paola did not seem visibly upset about this, but rather she somewhat accepted it as the norm. She continued, "So, I mean in the end I ended up working . . . and most of the people always are people that do good, but it started off with all stupid stuff." Additionally, when I asked Keiana what one of the things she was looking forward to the least in the following semester was, she said the "dating games" at the BSU officer meetings that the president holds at his house every week. "That's just one thing I don't like; I hate looking forward to helping him out with his dates. He can go to the [dance] clubs for that."

Finally, Laura, a former undocumented student and a member of ULS, described how her gender became salient while she sought advice from her club adviser, an academic counselor with the Latino center on campus:

> Patti's really great, I think also, just the fact that she's a woman too, a Latina, and she's been through it, that's why I kind of take her word more than other people. Like it's not the same as my [male] history professor telling me, "Well, you know I've been through it too." Yeah I know, it's different, though. I don't know, girls understand each other.

In addition to ULS, BSU and NAS had women advisers students often turned to for guidance and inspiration to continue with their work, academic and club related. They also turned to each other, expressing how each other "got it" because they were women who shared the same ethnicity and were in similar positions. In fact, most of the women in the same clubs were friends and often referred to one another in the interviews. They often made statements like, "You know how girls are" and "Women always talk," and they mentioned "female drama." For these women, gender and race were not something they could separate while they engaged in their leadership roles, another analysis that is also missing from Astin's (1984) involvement theory.

Intersectional Leadership

Womanism, along with CRT, allows one to honor the intersection between race and gender. It is with this intersectional, theoretical approach that I analyzed these women's responses to how race and gender affects them in their student organizations. For example, Christina served as president of PSU with Angela as vice president. Christina's term was tumultuous and took a physical, academic, and emotional toll on her. Serving as one of the few woman presidents in the club's history, coupled with the gendered attitudes her group members held on leadership, she decided not to run for a second term. When asked how, if at all, her racial or ethnic background affected how she led the group, her answer included an analysis of race and gender:

> Being Pilipino affects the way I lead since our culture is very patriarchal, like they always want the women to stay at home and be moms or nurses, never doctors. You have to be a nurse. So, I guess, as a woman it's kind of hard to get your point across and if you come across too strong they kind of see you as a "bitch" or somebody like that. It's hard being a Pilipina and being in a strong leadership position without getting branded with that title.

Here Christina talked about how her race and gender are intertwined in terms of leadership. According to her, Pilipina women are seen as serving in secondary supportive roles, such as a nurse, never as a doctor. This can be translated into a student organization as always being a secretary, never a president. However, Christina was a president, and according to her, a strong one. This came with consequences, such as being viewed as a "bitch." This derogatory term not only became gendered but also raced when directed toward her (Kleinman, Ezzell, & Frost, 2009). Christina said it was difficult being a Pilipina leader without being branded with that pejorative title in PSU.

Angela, Christina's vice president, agreed with this sentiment. Poised to be president after Christina's term, she turned down the nomination because she saw the toll it took on Christina and could no longer withstand the deficit views her club members held toward leadership. However, when asked if she would recommend other women to take a position in PSU, she said she would.

> For PSU, I think I would still tell people to be leaders, try to do something about it, especially for the women because I know in Pilipino traditions women are known to be submissive, to be under the man, staying at home all

the time to take care of the kids, but I think that's how it is for other cultures too. I know there were a lot of issues with women being taken for granted, seen as less as a human [than] men. So I think it's really important that women continue to take on these positions, to help them socially and I believe spiritually too. It helps them strengthen and gives the person growth.

For Angela, continuing to be visible and challenging the traditional views of Pilipina women were what led her to encourage other women to take on leadership positions in PSU. Although she stepped down from her nomination, she continued to be active in the club during the next semester.

CONCLUSION

The experiences of women community college student leaders of color on the transfer path are vital to include when discussing the racial disparities in the transfer function and the lack of people of color's voices in current theoretical leadership or involvement literature. The students in my study countered Astin's (1984) involvement theory in three ways: despite being community college students with multiple commitments they were still engaged with campus life and activities; even with high levels of involvement their persistence and academic success suffered; and this lack of persistence can be explained in how their experiences were filtered through a raced, classed, sexed, and gendered lens.

Many women of color feel the weight of the historical injustices faced by their communities, and the symbolic privilege associated with attending college reinforces their loyalty to their ethnic communities. Thus, their involvement at times can supersede their academic commitments, and they do not transfer to four-year colleges at the same rate as their White peers. This phenomenon becomes increasingly complex in a community college setting where students of color constitute the majority, and transferring to a four-year institution enables them to procure a bachelor's degree for a better chance at achieving economic and personal security.

Future theoretical frameworks concerning student development, leadership, and persistence should combine Astin's (1984) theory of involvement and build on it, not simply discard or debunk it. By using CRT and womanism to inform some of the shortcomings in student involvement theory, I believe I have taken the first steps toward this theoretical movement.

Faculty and staff at community colleges should be trained to work with student leaders and women-of-color student leaders in particular. Academic counselors could assist with readying these students to transfer by receiving specialized training that helps them recognize the delicate balance between the students' leadership and academic success. This training could be applied toward student leaders in general; however, as this study demonstrates, women-of-color student leaders experience involvement in a very raced and gendered way that comes with its own unique set of academic gains and consequences. However, in general, the traditional trope that all student leaders are academically adept needs to be abandoned. It is time for education professionals to reconceptualize the notion of involvement and to recognize that student leadership does not automatically equate with persistence or high academic achievement.

REFERENCES

Abrahamowicz, D. (1988). College involvement, perceptions, and satisfaction: A study of membership in student organizations. *Journal of College Student Development, 29*, 233–238.

American Association of Community Colleges. (2013). *2013 community college fast facts*. Retrieved from http://www.aacc.nche.edu/AboutCC/Documents/FactSheet2013.pdf

Arminio, J. L., Carter, S., Jones, S. E., Kruger, K., Lucas, N., Washington, J., . . . Scott, A. (2000). Leadership experiences of students of color. *NASPA Journal, 37*, 496–510.

Astin, A. W. (1984). Student involvement: A developmental theory for higher education. *Journal of College Student Personnel, 25*, 297–308.

Astin, A. W. (1999). Student involvement: A developmental theory for higher education. *Journal of College Student Development, 40*, 518–529.

Bailey, T., & Morest, V. S. (2006). *Defending the community college equity agenda*. Baltimore, MD: John Hopkins University Press.

Bernal, D. D. (1998). Grassroots leadership reconceptualized: Chicana oral histories and the 1968 East Los Angeles school blowouts. *Frontiers, 19*(2), 113–138.

Brint, S., & Karabel, J. (1989). *The diverted dream: Community colleges and the promise of educational opportunity in America, 1900–1985*. New York, NY: Oxford University Press.

California Community Colleges Chancellor's Office. (2013). *System strategic plan for the California community colleges: Preparing the foundation for California's future*.

Retrieved from http://californiacommunitycolleges.cccco.edu/Portals/0/reports TB/2013StrategicPlan_062013.pdf

Center for Community College Student Engagement. (2013). *About CCSSE: About the community college survey of student engagement.* Retrieved from http://www. ccsse.org/aboutccsse/aboutccsse.cfm

Chang, M. J. (2002). Racial dynamics on campus: What student organizations can tell us. *About Campus, 7*(1), 2–8.

Connor, A., & Griffith, M. (1994). *Democracy's open door: The community college in America's future.* Portsmouth, NH: Heinemann.

Creswell, J. W. (2002). *Research design: Qualitative, quantitative, and mixed methods approaches* (2nd ed.). Thousand Oaks, CA: Sage.

Delgado, R., & Stefancic, J. (2001). *Critical race theory: An introduction.* New York, NY: New York University Press.

Friedlander, J., Murrell, P. H., & MacDougall, P. R. (1993). The community college student experiences questionnaire. In T. W. Banta & Associates (Eds.), *Making a difference: Outcomes of a decade of assessment in higher education* (pp. 196–210). San Francisco, CA: Jossey-Bass.

Hagedorn, L. S., Moon, H. S., Cypers, S., Maxwell, W. E., & Lester, J. (2006). Transfer between community colleges and four-year colleges: The all-American game. *Community College Journal of Research and Practice, 30,* 223–242.

Harper, S. R., & Quaye, S. J. (2007). Student organizations as venues for Black identity expression and development among African American male student leaders. *Journal of College Student Development, 48*(2), 127–144.

Jain, D. (2009). *Women of color student leaders: The role of race and gender in community college transfer readiness* (Doctoral dissertation). Available from ProQuest Dissertations and Theses Database. (UMI No. 3405596)

Jain, D., & Turner, C. S. (2012). Purple is to lavender: Womanism, resistance, and the politics of naming. *Negro Educational Review, 62*(4), 67–88.

Kezar, A., & Moriarty, D. (2000). Expanding our understanding of student leadership development: A study exploring gender and ethnic identity. *Journal of College Student Development, 4*(1), 55–69.

Kleinman, S., Ezzell, M. B., & Frost, C. (2009). Reclaiming critical analysis: The social harms of "bitch." *Sociological Analysis, 3*(1), 47–68.

Ladson-Billings, G., & Tate, W. F. (1995). Toward a critical race theory of education. *Teachers College Record, 97*(1), 47–68.

Maxwell, J. A. (1996). *Qualitative research design: An interactive approach.* Thousand Oaks, CA: Sage.

Pascarella, E., & Terenzini, P. (2005). *How college affects students: Vol. 2, A third decade of research.* San Francisco, CA: Jossey-Bass.

Phillips, L. (Ed.). (2006). *The womanist reader*. New York, NY: Taylor & Francis.

Provasnik, S., & Planty, M. (2008). *Community colleges: Special supplement to the condition of education 2008* (NCES 2008-033). Washington, DC: National Center for Education Statistics, Institute of Education Sciences, U.S. Department of Education.

Rendón, L. I. (1993). Eyes on the prize: Students of color and the bachelor's degree. *Community College Review, 21*(2), 3–13.

Rendón, L. I., Jalomo, R. E., & Nora, A. (2000). Theoretical considerations in the study of minority student retention in higher education. In J. Braxton (Ed.), *Reworking the student departure puzzle* (pp. 127–156). Nashville, TN: Vanderbilt University Press.

Rhoads, R. A. (1998). *Freedom's web: Student activism in an age of cultural diversity*. Baltimore, MD: Johns Hopkins University Press.

Rhoads, R. A., & Valadez, J. R. (1996). *Democracy, multiculturalism, and the community college: A critical perspective*. New York, NY: Garland.

Solórzano, D. G. (1998). Critical race theory, race and gender microaggressions, and the experience of Chicana and Chicano scholars. *International Journal of Qualitative Studies in Education, 11*(1), 121–136.

Tinto, V. (1997). Classrooms as communities: Exploring the educational character of student persistence. *The Journal of Higher Education, 68*(6), 599–623.

Walker, A. (1983). *In search of our mothers' gardens*. New York, NY: Harcourt Brace Jovanovich.

Wassmer, R., Moore, C., & Shulock, N. (2004). The effect of racial/ethnic composition on transfer rates in community colleges: Implications for policy and practice. *Research in Higher Education, 45*, 651–672.

12

Looking Across the Research

Social and Cultural Capital's Interplay
With Marginalized Student Communities

Jesse S. Watson and Elizabeth Cox Brand

O VER THE COURSE OF THEIR EXISTENCE, American community colleges had many names, such as junior colleges, city colleges, technical institutes, and even democracy's colleges. One term in particular, *people's college*, coined by Cohen and Brawer (1996), paints the picture of a campus where everyone is accepted and educated. Unfortunately, that does not end up being the reality or experience for many students such as those with differing racial groups, genders, classes, social statuses, and sexual orientations; those with varying levels of physical or academic ability; or military veterans. The resulting environment may be one in which negative stereotypes abound and nondominant groups experience marginalization. Harbour and Ebie (2011) stated, "Student marginalization occurs at times when [and] where and [in] places students are most vulnerable, that is, when they are seeking help and guidance from others" (p. 7). Studies regarding marginalized groups in higher education have generally focused on underrepresented minority groups or those with differing levels of physical ability. We certainly acknowledge the challenges these groups may face in postsecondary education; however, we sought to expand the notion of marginalized groups, particularly in the community college setting.

SOCIAL AND CULTURAL CAPITAL

Dominant groups whose values and norms are centric on campus play out through various forms of capital, which influence and further exacerbate the marginalization experienced by multiple types of minority groups. Capital in the broadest economic sense can take time to accumulate and has the capacity to "produce profits and to reproduce itself in identical or expanded form" (Bourdieu, 1986, p. 241). Yosso (2005) summarized Bourdieu's *capital* as being "the knowledge of the upper and middle classes, [which is] considered capital valuable to a hierarchical society" (p. 70). Yosso later noted that privileged groups in our society treasure these forms of knowledge accumulation. Understanding capital as something that can be amassed and brings benefits to the possessor is key as we move into more discrete forms of capital, such as cultural and social capital.

Cultural capital, as described by Bourdieu (1986), is "convertible, on certain occasions, into economic capital and may be institutionalized in the form of educational qualifications" (p. 243). Cultural capital is intangible and can lead or assist an individual in acquiring tangible items such as access to an institution of higher education or successful navigation of standardized testing. It provides the possessor with a tool chest of sorts used for personal gain. "Any given cultural competence (e.g., being able to read in a world of illiterates) derives a scarcity value from its position in the distribution of cultural capital and yields profits of distinction for its owner" (Bourdieu, 1986, p. 243). Cultural capital is also a commodity passed along within groups and requires a supportive network for it to replicate itself in a group, similar to bequeathing wealth from one generation to another; the example in higher education is the legacy practices in college admissions.

Social capital, as discussed by Bourdieu (1986), is "made up of social obligations (connections), which [are] convertible, in certain conditions, into economic capital and may be institutionalized in the form of a title of nobility" (p. 243). Adler and Kwon (2000) added that social capital is a resource created by the configuration and content of the network of their more or less durable social relations. Burt (2000) talked about *social capital* as being "a metaphor in which social structure is a kind of capital that can create for certain individuals or groups a competitive advantage in pursuing their ends. Better connected people enjoy higher returns" (p. 348). This last point resonates with us most because it ties together all aspects of social capital. The majority group positions those advantaged individuals who possess connections to further their returns, which could be monetary, access to higher education, or equitable treatment.

MARGINALIZED COMMUNITIES

The term *marginal* is applied to a variety of groups, organizations, or even circumstances. However, it is agreed that the use of the term produces negative stereotypes toward minority groups. Membership in these marginalized groups is relegated to those seen as *other*—those excluded from the mainstream of society. Harbour and Ebie (2011) stated, "Student marginalization might be embedded in a variety of individual behaviors, institutional policies, and social or cultural practices that attack students on a very personal level" (p. 7). Historically, this has included those of different races, religions, or physical abilities and has more recently expanded to those of differing sexual orientations or social class. Unfortunately, such stereotyping permeates society and is present in higher education. In fact, as Rhoads (1995) stated, some feel that "issues of race, gender, class, and sexual orientation have become central to what some see as fragmentation within today's academe" (p. 5).

Ever since the founding of Joliet Junior College in 1901, community colleges have occupied a subordinate status to senior, four-year institutions. Expanding marginalization to the institutional level, community colleges are on the periphery of the higher education landscape. Not only does this seem to be prominent in the minds of many in higher education, but as Townsend and LaPaglia (2000) found, many who are part of community colleges as faculty and administrators also believe that their institutions are held in low regard in academe. Perhaps Barry and Barry (1992) said it best when stating, "Community colleges are prisoners of elitism with little chance of escape" (p. 43).

COMMUNITY COLLEGE CONTEXT

American community colleges have been referred to by various names, as previously mentioned, with our preferred designation being Cohen and Brawer's (2008) "people's college" (p. 5). The implication is consistent with the mission of community colleges, which is to provide access for all community members to postsecondary education. Statistics bear this out as community colleges serve 45% of all undergraduates in the United States including large numbers of minority student populations: 56% Hispanic, 49% Black, 42% Native American, and 44% Asian/Pacific Islander (American Association of Community Colleges [AACC], 2013).

Along with race and ethnicity, other characteristics describe the more than 12 million community college students in the United States. Despite increases in enrollments of younger students, community college students continue to be older than the traditional direct-from-high-school student; the average age of a community college student today is 28 years (AACC, 2013). Students who work greater numbers of hours are more likely to attend a community college than a four-year institution (Joshi & Nsiah, 2009). In fact, 59% of full-time and 47% of part-time community college students are employed part-time (AACC, 2013). Adding to the complexity of this mix, 40% of community college students are the first generation in their families to attend college (AACC, 2013). All these factors combined may inhibit a student's ability to persist (Levin, 2007) and be successful in her or his educational endeavors.

Despite these factors, with the exception of 2011–2012, enrollments at community colleges have been increasing for years and show no signs of slowing. According to the AACC (2013), enrollments at community colleges decreased 3% between fall 2011 and fall 2012. As the numbers and diversity of community college enrollments grow, community college faculty, staff, and administrators play a greater role in educating students of the United States (Joshi & Nsiah, 2009). As Laden (2004) noted, "At the beginning of the twenty-first century, community colleges continue to exemplify historical American core values of providing educational access and opportunity to all citizens and residents" (p. 1). This idea of providing access and opportunity for the surrounding community has created multiple missions for community colleges. Unlike their four-year counterparts, whose primary mission is to provide academic education for baccalaureate attainment and beyond, community college administrators and faculty work to provide curricula to fulfill all the educational needs of their stakeholders. These needs may include highly technical training for local business and industry, developmental classes for those underprepared for college course work, and courses designed for transfer to a baccalaureate program—all within one institution. Although it may seem that with all they do to serve their constituents community colleges would be highly valued, this often is not the case; these multidimensional, responsive institutions are relegated to the periphery of academe. In this dynamic campus context, we examine groups of marginalized students who are cast to the outskirts of postsecondary education.

A VIEW FROM THE COMMUNITY COLLEGE PERIPHERY

To be a *community* college the institution must meet the needs of those within a designated service area. In this capacity, community colleges have arguably the most diverse enrollments in higher education because of open access, which makes the community college student population extremely varied. On any given community college campus, one may find English-as-a-second-language (ESL) learners, students taking remedial courses, and students seeking to transfer to a four-year institution. The following is an analysis of four articles from a *New Directions for Community Colleges* (Cox & Watson, 2011) issue with specific application of the concepts of social and cultural capital. The marginalized populations include ESL learners; student athletes; lesbian, gay, bisexual, transgender, and queer (LGBTQ) students; and veterans.

In a study of adult immigrant ESL learners making the transition from noncredit to credit programs in a California community college, Becker (2011) examined those who were marginalized in their home countries because of weak educational backgrounds, low socioeconomic status, and negligible employment opportunities. These students faced a more difficult path to achieving their personal and professional goals in the United States than their peers who possessed higher levels of capital. In fact, even though these individuals may have made positive strides in some areas of their lives, such as in the workplace, marginalization was still present in their roles as students. "Although they had gained self-confidence and cultural capital in the workplace—particularly in comparison with coworkers who had not invested time in learning English—participants with low cultural capital still expressed a sense of marginality within the academic setting" (Becker, 2011, p. 16). Even with developing an effective use of English, these students felt they did not possess the capital necessary to be successful in higher education.

The experience of adult immigrant ESL learners in community colleges is an explicit example of cultural and social capital. Unlike other groups featured in Becker's (2011) article, adult immigrant ESL learners are unique in that they have left behind any capital they may have had in their home countries to move to the United States. The students in Becker's study start with a deficit of capital because of their international, academic, and professional transitions. Compared to their collegiate peers, they have a shortage of relevant cultural and social capital because of their position as immigrants and ESL learners in a foreign system. Having to begin the accumulation process from scratch challenges them in ways that are inconceivable to their domestic peers as they navigate the avenues of employment, education, and the larger society.

Student athletes are not typically considered a marginalized group because of their institutional status. A very public and high-profile position on campus may lead one to believe that these students have no issues in their campus lives. However, Horton (2011) found that the status accorded to these students via their position on campus may create distress and even obstacles in student athletes' educational journeys. Student athletes have been confronted with the negative stereotype of the "dumb jock" who is lazy and interested in college only so he or she can play sports (Horton, 2011, p. 27). This disapproving image may lower expectations from faculty and the institution, causing underachievement in student athletes academically and socially.

Horton (2011) pointed out how student athletes face marginalization as they enjoy high social status in some aspects of their lives but are estranged in others; for example, student athletes receive continual praise for their athletic performance in sports but are also criticized for their unsatisfactory academic performance. "As such, student athletes are confronted with layered marginalization due to their status as a community college student, student athlete, and when applicable, as a member of an under-represented ethnic, gender or socio-economic group" (Horton, 2011, p. 29).

Student athletes are an interesting group in regard to capital because they represent a capital paradox. In one respect, their contextual campus status provides them with a high level of cultural and social capital based on their physical prowess and sports-related accomplishments. Examples of such capital are access to higher education; accolades from their peers, faculty, and staff; and perks from the surrounding community, such as interviews in newspapers and public admiration. Conversely, athletes as described by Horton (2011) can simultaneously experience marginalization because of stereotypes regarding their academic focus and achievement abilities. The negative connotations result in a reduced amount of social capital in the academic environment by their being viewed as underachievers or unintelligent by campus constituents.

Community colleges are the melting pot of American higher education as they welcome students who span the ranges in races and ethnicities, academic abilities, and socioeconomic statuses. Yet scholars have found that for a particular student population—sexual minority students—this pluralistic campus environment is not only marginalizing but also openly harassing and at times violent. LGBTQ students face the "hostile hallways that exist at two-year institutions" (Zamani-Gallaher & Choudhuri, 2011, p. 38).

The literature base focusing on LGBTQ students at community colleges documented by Zamani-Gallaher and Choudhuri (2011) was found to be lacking in breadth and depth. Therefore, not only are LGBTQ students being marginalized in our campus hallways, classrooms, and surrounding communities, they are being marginalized in our academic literature as well. These students are spurned covertly with glances, stares, and whispers but also overtly through campus laws that ban gay rights events and memorials and by the lack of institutional support for the LGBTQ community.

LGBTQ students have compounding effects of capital because their marginalized status arises from their sexual orientation or identity, which is affected by their other capital-accumulating statuses such as race, socioeconomic status, and gender. The cultural and social capital LGBTQ students may possess based on their varying statuses may give them many advantages, such as access to higher education, monetary benefits, and membership in the majority community. However, when their LGBTQ status is announced or known by the community at large, such information may negatively affect their cache of capital because they may be shunned by peers or institutional staff, be penalized by familial members socially or monetarily, or experience elevated personal safety fears while out in the surrounding community.

Rounding out the discussion are student veterans, who after completing their military service and tours of duty choose to use their educational benefits and pursue postsecondary education, as discussed in Chapter 10. Student veterans have been present on college campuses since the passage of the Servicemen's Readjustment Act of 1944 (more commonly known as the GI Bill; DVA, n.d). The Gulf War and military campaigns in Afghanistan coupled with an economic downturn have caused an increase in the number of veterans seeking postsecondary education (Rumann, Rivera, & Hernandez, 2011). Factors such as proximity to home, flexible class schedules, and older student populations have made the community college a very attractive postsecondary option for student veterans. Again, with financial support, such as tuition covered by their service benefits, one may think that these individuals would have few concerns in the role of a student. However, studies have found that student veterans may often conceal their military identities because they are concerned about how they may be perceived by others, and this affects their interpersonal treatment (Rumann et al., 2011).

Rumann et al. (2011) found that veterans returning to campus might face an environment that is quite marginalizing. Nonmilitary peers may foster a climate of otherness and exploitation when asking student veterans questions regarding their experiences, such as, "How many people did you kill over there?" Faculty members may be perceived as unsupportive because of antiwar comments they make in class; others in the campus community may voice derogatory opinions about military operations. All these experiences lead to a negative impact on student veterans, further encouraging them to disengage and withdraw from the social and academic environment.

Veteran students are similar to ESL students in that they move to a different culture (i.e., the military environment to the civilian environment) from the one they have become accustomed to with certain processes and amassed amounts of unusable cultural and social capital. They are also similar to student athletes and LGBTQ students because they can choose to withhold revealing the military background in their personal identities. Taking the stance as a transplant from another culture, veteran students must first become accustomed to the new processes of the civilian world and then begin the cultural and social capital acquisition process. The perceptions of veterans and political viewpoints of others may affect social interactions, which may also be exacerbated by any personal effects encumbered during service-related experiences, potentially leading to a negative impact on their academic persistence.

It is important to note that although we re-represent these marginalized student groups as individual populations on community college campuses, these students have multiple identities. Normative systemic powers exist on campus, playing out in multiple ways, such as gender (male dominance), sexual orientation (heterosexism), race (normative Whiteness), class (upper- and middle-class values), military service (graphic combat and related stigmas), and athletes (false assumptions about intellectual ability). The parenthetical dominant values highlight why the identities of our featured community college students are marginalized and made to be "Other." Without a normative systemic power, in many forms these groups of students would not be considered marginal. "Students may also be marginalized as a result of institutional policies or practices that intentionally or unintentionally subordinate students because of their status or identity" (Harbour & Ebie, 2011, p. 7).

CONCLUSION

The acquisition and accumulation of cultural and social capital is a systemic artifact that benefits the majority of centered groups whether based on race, gender, sexual orientation, or class. Harbour and Ebie (2011) cited Hardiman and Jackson when defining the *marginalization of students* as being "subordinated, discounted, or ignored because of their status or identity by individual behaviors, institutional policies and practices, and social beliefs and conditions that they cannot control" (p. 7). The goal is to illuminate how marginalization can take many shapes and how it directly affects the accumulation and use of cultural and social capital by individuals who are marginalized.

The following recommendations are intended to assist institution administrators and campus-based personnel with introducing concepts of capital to marginalized students and assisting with obtaining the connections needed to develop cultural and social capital:

◆ Support and expand the scope and depth of summer bridge programs so that incoming students are aware of the concepts of capital and how they affect the daily lives of students.

◆ Provide curriculum-supported seminars, brown-bag sessions, and campuswide presentations that focus on the development and compilation of social and cultural capital for marginalized students.

◆ Develop and foster peer-to-peer and staff mentor relationships along with on-campus connections so that individuals can be exposed to experiential, day-to-day capital building.

◆ Encourage student organizations and events that support marginalized populations and build capital by publicly demonstrating that all people are valued and integral parts of the campus community.

◆ Require professional development training for administrators, staff, and faculty regarding the unique needs and challenges of marginalized populations so they will be knowledgeable about how to help students recognize, develop, and use social and cultural capital.

◆ Make contact with the people in students' support networks to educate them on the academic process and subsequent demands placed on students by meeting these groups on their turf and carrying out presentations at local community centers.

◆ Create an institutional commitment to combat capital accumulation deficits through education-based efforts such as safe space discussion groups that highlight personal identity and the meaning of being marginalized.

◆ Use local resources by inviting people from local and regional organizations, activist groups, successful members of the community, and faculty and staff researchers from surrounding colleges and universities to speak.

Community colleges will continue their legacy of enrolling students of diverse social classes, academic abilities, sexual orientations, and genders. As part of the mission to serve their students, community college administrators, faculty, and staff must work with the entire institution to develop learning communities that are inclusive if they are to help students "fulfill the American dream" (Vaughan, 1985, p. 28).

REFERENCES

Adler, P. S., & Kwon, S. W. (2000). Social capital: The good, the bad, and the ugly. In E. L. Lesser (Ed.), *Knowledge and social capital: Foundations and applications* (pp. 89–118). Boston, MA: Butterworth-Heinemann.

American Association of Community Colleges. (2013). *2013 community college fact sheet.* Retrieved from http://www.aacc.nche.edu/AboutCC/Pages/fastfactsfactsheet.aspx

Barry, R. J., & Barry, P. A. (1992). Establishing equity in the articulation process. *New Directions for Community Colleges*, (78), 35–44.

Becker, L. A. (2011). Noncredit to credit transitioning matters for adult ESL learners in a California community college. *New Directions for Community Colleges*, (155), 15–26.

Bourdieu, P. (1986). The forms of capital. In J. G. Richardson (Ed.), *Handbook of theory and research for the sociology of education* (pp. 241–258). New York, NY: Greenwood Press.

Burt, R. S. (2000). The network structure of social capital. In B. M. Staw & R. I. Sutton (Eds.), *Research in organizational behavior* (pp. 345–423). Danvers, MA: Elsevier.

Cohen, A. M., & Brawer, F. B. (2008). *The American community college* (5th ed.). San Francisco, CA: Jossey-Bass.

Cox, E. M., & Watson, J. S. (Eds.). (2011). Marginalized students. *New Directions for Community Colleges*, (155).

Harbour, C. P., & Ebie, G. (2011). A Deweyan perspective on student marginalization at the community college. *New Directions for Community Colleges*, (155), 5–14.

Horton, D., Jr. (2011). Developing an institutional culture toward degree attainment for student athletes. *New Directions for Community Colleges*, (155), 27–33.

Joshi, P. V., & Nsiah, C. (2009). Student characteristics affecting the decision to enroll in a community college: Economic rationale and empirical evidence. *Community College Journal of Research and Practice, 33*, 805–822.

Laden, B. V. (Ed.). (2004). Serving emerging majority students. *New Directions for Community Colleges*, (127), 5–19.

Levin, J. S. (2007). *Non-traditional students and community colleges: The conflict of justice and neo-liberalism.* New York, NY: Palgrave Macmillan.

Rhoads, R. A. (1995, April). *Multiculturalism and border knowledge in higher education.* Paper presented at the annual meeting of the American Educational Research Association, San Francisco, CA.

Rumann, C. B., Rivera, M., & Hernandez, I. (2011). Student veterans and community colleges. *New Directions for Community Colleges*, (155), 51–58.

Townsend, B. K., & LaPaglia, N. (2000). Are we marginalized within academe? Perceptions of two-year college faculty. *Community College Review*, 28(1), 41–48.

U.S. Department of Veterans Affairs (n.d.). *Education and training: History and timeline.* Retrieved from http://www.benefits.va.gov/gibill/history.asp

Vaughan, G. B. (1985). Maintaining open access and comprehensiveness. *New Directions for Community Colleges*, (52), 17–28.

Yosso, T. J. (2005). Whose culture has capital? A critical race theory discussion of community cultural wealth. *Race Ethnicity and Education*, 8(1), 69–91.

Zamani-Gallaher, E. M., & Choudhuri, D. D. (2011). A primer on LGBTQ students at community colleges: Considerations for research and practice *New Directions for Community Colleges*, (155), 35–49.

Afterword

Stephanie R. Bulger

T HERE IS LITTLE DOUBT that American community colleges are at a crossroads. Funding systems are out of whack. Graduation rates are being scrutinized. Technology is producing disruptive innovations. College readiness is a well-intentioned pursuit, and job preparedness is a murky concept. Situated in this complex, diverse, educational, economic, legal, technological, and regulatory environment, community colleges are rapidly searching for better ways to serve students.

This timely volume recognizes our urgent need for new strategies. The chapters are an important addition to addressing the needs of students in our institutions in a broader historic, economic, and public policy context. Coeditors Kelsay and Zamani-Gallaher have assembled a phenomenal group of researchers, higher education faculty, college presidents, and community college administrators to review current challenges and issues facing community colleges with a refreshing focus on assisting community college students who may come from backgrounds that are socially, educationally, or economically disadvantaged. The editors and contributors do exceptionally well in delving deeply into the questions we ask ourselves about these students but with few reference points to create programs and services that will contribute to their success.

The contributors' research and analysis give us a thorough understanding of students who have received scant attention in higher education literature, including the undocumented, displaced, and foreign born; older adult learners; and military veterans. We not only learn about the barriers our institutions have erected (albeit unintentional) but are also given specific ways we can ease these students' transition into college and through the maze of the college experience to completion. These chapters further challenge our assumptions about the correlation between leadership experiences and

171

academic success and expand our definitions of student subgroups, which we tend to paint as monolithic or simply ignore.

The additional value of this comprehensive book is that community college administrators can discover how emerging strategies are working in institutions while planning pilot projects and before implementing costly programs. New frameworks and copious examples are offered for innovative retention strategies such as residence hall and orientation programs.

By moving the discussion to broader institutional levels, this compilation provides community college administrators with advice on their organizational culture and institutional outcomes as well. Acknowledging the silo effect of departments in many community colleges, the contributors provide persuasive arguments for eliminating this effect in student and academic affairs departments. The convincing strategies presented by the authors suggest that departments that collaborate to strengthen the academic and social engagement of students will enhance today's student success agendas in community colleges. In Chapter 4, the authors argue that community colleges have a responsibility for increasing technological literacy in our communities in a postindustrial world. They encourage us to view the technological literacy of faculty and students as a core competency necessary for teaching in community colleges, working in today's occupations, and thriving as a student in colleges and universities.

The backdrop of this volume is the future of community colleges. The first section of this book lays out the evolution of community colleges and their centrality today to the economic vitality of our nation in a complex social, economic, and political environment. Again, the real experiences of the diverse students who attend community colleges are the focus. Although the future is hopeful, the contributors are cautiously optimistic about our ability to fulfill our comprehensive mission in the current climate.

The eye-opening chapters in this volume cause me to be optimistic as well. As a community college educator in a multicampus, urban-suburban college with more than 15 years of experience in leadership roles and teaching, I am buoyed by the strategies, recommendations, best practices, and advice from the contributors. These solutions are a way for faculty, administrators, presidents, and board members to discuss, debate, tweak, and try.

I commend the members of ACPA–College Student Educators International's Commission for Two-Year Colleges for their foresight in supporting this important work. It sheds light on the students who are not often represented in the higher education literature to help those on the margins of society achieve full participation in higher education. I believe they have accomplished this goal.

Once in a while, a book forces us to reconsider the fundamentals of our practices and that book is this one. This volume fills a void in the current literature and is a must-read for anyone struggling to understand today's dilemmas in community colleges. It informs and prepares graduate students in higher education administration, counseling, and student affairs programs. Faculty and graduate students can build on research questions introduced in this volume (e.g., see Chapter 5 on diverse students, Chapter 9 on the older adult learner, Chapter 10 on veterans, Chapter 11 on women students of color in leadership, and Chapter 12 on marginalized communities). This volume is an indispensable tool in the administrator's tool kit and will be well used as we go boldly into the future.

Additional Resources

Tamara N. Stevenson

PROFESSIONAL ORGANIZATIONS

ACPA Commission for Two-Year Colleges
http://www2.myacpa.org/twoyear-home

American Association for Women in Community Colleges
http://www.aawccnatl.org

American Association of Community Colleges
http://www.aacc.nche.edu

Association of College and University Housing Officers–International
http://www.acuho-i.org

Council for the Advancement of Standards in Higher Education
http://www.cas.edu

Council for the Study of Community Colleges
http://www.cscconline.org

National Academic Advising Association Two-Year Colleges Commission
http://www.nacada.ksu.edu/Community/Commission-Interest-Groups/
Institutional-Type/Two-Year-Colleges-Commission.aspx

National Community College Council for Research and Planning
http://www.ncccrp.org

National Community College Hispanic Council
http://www.ncchc.com

National Council on Student Development
http://www.ncsdonline.org/home/index.html

Student Affairs Administrators in Higher Education, Community College Division
http://www.naspa.org/divctr/ccdiv/default.cfm

WEB RESOURCES

Association for the Orientation, Transition, and Retention in Higher Education Two-Year College Network
http://www.nodaweb.org

Center for Community College Student Engagement
http://www.ccsse.org/center/

Center for Global Advancement for Community Colleges
http://www.cgacc.org

Community College Consortium for Immigrant Education
http://www.cccie.org

Community College Research Center
http://ccrc.tc.columbia.edu

Community College Week: The Independent Voice Serving Community, Technical, and Junior Colleges
http://www.ccweek.com

Complete College America
http://www.completecollege.org

Consortium of Higher Education LGBT Resource Professionals
http://www.lgbtcampus.org

Council for Adult and Experiential Learning
http://www.cael.org/home

Council for Opportunity in Education
http://www.coenet.us

Council for the Advancement and Support of Education
http://www.case.org

¡Excelencia! in Education (Latino/Latina Students)
http://www.edexcelencia.org

National Institution for the Study of Transfer Students
http://blog.ung.edu/transferinstitute/

Office of Community College Research and Leadership
http://occrl.illinois.edu

PUBLICATIONS

ACT. (2013). *The reality of college readiness 2013: National.* Retrieved from http://www.act.org/readinessreality/13/pdf/Reality-of-College-Readiness-2013.pdf

American Association of Community Colleges. (2012, April). *Reclaiming the American dream: A report from the 21st-Century Commission on the Future of Community Colleges.* Retrieved from http://www.aacc.nche.edu/21stCenturyReport

American Association of University Women. (2013). *Women in community colleges: Access to success.* Retrieved from http://www.aauw.org/files/2013/05/women-in-community-colleges.pdf

American College Counseling Association. (2013). *Community college task force survey 2012–2013.* Alexandria, VA: Author.

Century Foundation. (2013). *Bridging the higher education divide: Strengthening community colleges and restoring the American dream.* Retrieved from http://tcf.org/assets/downloads/20130523-Bridging_the_Higher_Education_Divide-REPORT-ONLY.pdf

Johnson, L., Adams Becker, S., Cummins, M., Estrada, V., Freeman, A., & Ludgate, H. (2013). *Technology outlook for community, technical, and junior colleges 2013–2018: An NMC Horizon Project sector analysis.* Retrieved from http://www.nmc.org/pdf/2013-technology-outlook-community-colleges.pdf

Rath, B., Rock, K., & Laferriere, A. (2013). *Pathways through college: Strategies for improving community college student success.* Retrieved from http://www.opp.org/docs/PathwaysCollegeStrategies_StudentSuccess.pdf

Santiago, D., & Stettner, A. (2013). *Supporting Latino community college students: An investment in our economic future.* Retrieved from http://www.edexcelencia.org/sites/default/files/excelencia_singlestop_slccs_report.pdf

Editors and Contributors

EDITORS

LISA S. KELSAY is assistant dean of liberal arts and director of academic arts at Moraine Valley Community College in Illinois. She is also a part-time instructor in education at the college and an adjunct professor in the Graduate School at Kaplan University. She holds a PhD in higher education from Loyola University Chicago, an MA in student personnel administration in higher education from Ball State University, and a BS in education from the University of Akron. For more than 15 years, Kelsay has worked in student and academic affairs, at private and public institutions, and at two-year and four-year colleges. Her research has been published in *The Journal of College Admission*, and she was the recipient of the 2013 ACPA Commission for Two-Year Colleges Service to the Profession Award. She served as the 2009–2012 chair of the ACPA Commission for Two-Year Colleges.

EBONI M. ZAMANI-GALLAHER is professor of educational leadership and coordinator of the Community College Leadership Program in the Department of Leadership and Counseling at Eastern Michigan University. She holds a PhD in higher education administration with a specialization in community college leadership and educational evaluation from the University of Illinois at Urbana–Champaign. Zamani-Gallaher's teaching, research, and consulting activities largely include psychosocial adjustment and transition of marginalized collegians, transfer, access policies, women in leadership, and institutional practices affecting work and family balance. Her work includes cowriting *The Case for Affirmative Action on Campus: Concepts of Equity, Considerations for Practice* (Sterling, VA: Stylus, 2009), coediting *African American Females: Addressing Challenges and Nurturing the Future* (Lansing: Michigan State University Press, 2013), and *The State of the African American Male (Courageous Conversations)* (Lansing: Michigan State University

Press, 2010). She is coeditor of *ASHE Reader on Organization & Governance in Higher Education* (6th ed., Boston, MA: Pearson Publications, 2010) and *ASHE Reader on Community Colleges* (4th ed., Boston, MA: Pearson Publications, in press). Zamani-Gallaher is president of the Council for the Study of Community Colleges, an affiliate of the American Association of Community Colleges.

CONTRIBUTORS

CARIN W. BARBER received her doctorate in educational leadership from Eastern Michigan University. She earned a master's degree in educational leadership and policy studies and a bachelor of science degree in marketing education from Virginia Polytechnic Institute and State University (Virginia Tech). Barber is an adjunct assistant professor of education in educational policy, planning, and leadership at the College of William and Mary. Barber has worked in residence life at Eastern Michigan University, Southern Methodist University, and Virginia Tech.

CHRISTOPHER BONAPACE is a graduate of the master's educational leadership program with a specialization in student affairs administration at Eastern Michigan University. He is the Student Success Specialist for the culinary program of Dorsey Schools in Roseville, Michigan. He has previously worked in the financial aid department at Dorsey Schools and in academic advising at Eastern Michigan University. His professional background includes work as a rehabilitation technician for individuals with neurological disorders and as a therapeutic horseback riding instructor for individuals with special needs. His research interests include the psychosocial benefits of therapeutic horseback riding for older adult learners and assessing student outcomes in alignment with organizational culture.

STEPHANIE R. BULGER is the district vice chancellor of educational affairs of the Wayne County Community College District, an urban-suburban multi-campus institution that serves more than 72,000 students. Bulger has published "The Win-Win of Exporting Distance Learning" in *Community College Journal* (Washington, DC: American Association of Community Colleges, 2005), *Who Owns What: Current Policy and Practice Regarding Online Course Ownership in Community Colleges* (Washington, DC: Instructional Technology Council, 2008), and "Using Technology to Reach and Serve the New

Student Diversity" in *Reinventing the Open Door: Transformational Strate-gies for Community Colleges* (Washington, DC: Community College Press, 2010). She is the editorial director of *Great Leadership*, a national newsletter distributed to more than 1,100 community colleges in the nation. Bulger serves as a consultant-evaluator for the Higher Learning Commission, is on the executive board of the Michigan AEC Women's Network, and has been on the advisory board of the National University Technology Network. She earned her doctorate in higher education from the University of Michigan. Bulger received the Distinguished Woman in Higher Education Leader-ship Award from the Michigan ACE Women's Network.

ELIZABETH COX BRAND is the director of research and communications for the Oregon Department of Community Colleges and Workforce Development. She received her PhD in educational leadership and policy studies from Iowa State University. Her research interests include marginalized populations, the role of gender in community colleges, and the experiences of adult com-munity college students. Cox Brand coedited a special themed issue of *New Directions for Community Colleges* focused on marginalized populations in community colleges.

SHAFTONE DUNKLIN is a higher education consultant for the state of Michi-gan's Veterans' Services Division. Dunklin is a veteran of the U.S. Marine Corps and currently assists educational and training institutions in gaining approval to certify veterans for federal benefits. Dunklin is a graduate of Slippery Rock University, where he received his BS in elementary education and his MA in college student personnel. He earned his PhD in educational leadership with a specialization in community college leadership from East-ern Michigan University.

TARA FAGAN has served as a counselor at Suffolk County Community College for over 10 years and worked in the field of higher education for 15 years. She completed a master of counselor education degree in 1997 from Long Island University and a master of social work degree in 2010 from the State University of New York at Stony Brook. Her research interests have focused on military veterans and their transition to college life. She completed a year-long sabbatical working at the Northport Veterans Affairs Medical Center during the 2009–2010 year that included clinical-level social work training in the center's Operation Enduring Freedom/Operation Iraqi Freedom Combat Office and the Mental Health Intensive Case Management program.

JESSICA HALE is a faculty member in the academic skills department at Washtenaw Community College in Ann Arbor, Michigan. Prior to working with transitioning students in the classroom, Hale coordinated the college's orientation program, welcoming more than 15,000 students to the campus, and participated in the development and implementation of a successful online orientation. For three years, she served as cochair of the Two-Year College Network of the National Orientation Directors Association. She has made presentations at national and international conferences on topics related to orientation, educational technology, and transitional programming for students and parents. Hale has published works in *The Review of Higher Education*, *The Journal of College Orientation and Transition*, and *The Orientation Review*. She holds an MA in higher education from the University of Michigan and completed her EdD in educational leadership at Eastern Michigan University.

DIMPAL JAIN is an assistant professor in educational leadership and policy studies in the Michael D. Eisner College of Education at California State University, Northridge. With over a decade of experience in student affairs, she has worked with community college students at two- and four-year colleges. She has fulfilled multiple roles throughout her career, including serving as a staff member at Seattle Central Community College; a researcher with the Center for Community College Partnerships at the University of California, Los Angeles; and a faculty member at Santa Monica College. Her research interests center broadly on issues related to race and racism in higher education; women leaders of color; the transfer function, including the creation of a transfer-receptive culture at the four-year college; and community colleges as raced and gendered institutions. She draws on the theoretical frameworks of critical race theory and womanism throughout her work. By using these frameworks, she attempts to dispel the narrative that community colleges are color blind and politically neutral, while recognizing the failure of the democratic promise of academic transfer from two-year to four-year colleges.

JOHN L. JAMROGOWICZ, who has spent almost 23 years at Trident Technical College in Charleston, South Carolina, has been dean of enrollment management since 2003, an office whose functions include admissions, financial aid/veterans assistance, orientation, registrar duties, and testing services. His experiences there have also included counseling, career development, disabilities services, and TRIO grant administration. Prior to arriving at Trident,

Jamrogowicz worked in residential life at the University of South Carolina and at Adams State College in Colorado. He also worked in residential life at three Job Corps centers in New England. John holds a BA in political science and an MEd in student personnel services, both from the University of South Carolina.

CORINNE KOWPAK has served at five different higher education institutions in the past 40 years. Her career began at the University of Vermont, where she was assistant or associate dean of students for most of her 17 years there. In 1990 Kowpak became the senior student affairs officer at Springfield College in Massachusetts. After eight years, she returned to her native New York to serve as vice president for enrollment management and student development at York College/City University of New York. In 2000 Kowpak became vice president for student affairs at Keene State College in New Hampshire. She was named dean of students at York County Community College in Maine in 2008. Kowpak was a first-generation college student who earned her BA in physical education at Hunter College of the City University of New York and completed her MEd and EdD degrees at the University of Vermont.

RAMONA MERAZ LEWIS is an assistant professor and faculty coordinator for the Higher Education Student Affairs Leadership Program in the educational leadership, research, and technology department at Western Michigan University. Her research interests focus on older adult learning in two- and four-year postsecondary contexts, college student learning and development with an emphasis on the over-50 learner, and qualitative methods. Prior to joining the university, Lewis served in a variety of student and academic affairs positions in residence life, student activities, first-year experience, academic advising, academic support services, and faculty development. She earned an EdD in educational leadership with a concentration in student affairs administration and gerontology from Eastern Michigan University and an MA in college student personnel from Bowling Green State University.

MARTHA MAZEIKA works in administration positions at community colleges that focus primarily on student success and retention. After completing a master of education degree in counseling and psychological services with a concentration in student personnel administration in 2000 from Springfield College, she started working at Springfield Technical Community College as director of adult basic education transitions, then as an academic counselor for a grant initiative funded by Title III. In 2006 she entered the doctoral program in community college leadership at Old Dominion University in Norfolk, Virginia, and is currently writing a dissertation that defines student success from the community college student perspective. Previously, she worked as the Director for Student Success Interventions at Moraine Valley Community College collaborating with academic and student affairs to enhance the infrastructure of student success and retention at the college.

CARA W. MCFADDEN is assistant professor of sport and event management at Elon University. She teaches the introductory course as well as research methods for the department. She received her PhD in educational leadership and policy studies with an emphasis in higher education from Virginia Tech. Her MA in recreation administration is from Central Michigan University. McFadden's research interests include psychosocial identity development of college students, instrument development and validation methods, and engaged learning environments.

PATRICIA MUNSCH has been working at Suffolk County Community College for 10 years. She is a counselor who has worked in the Office of Campus Activities and Student Leadership Development and the Counseling and Advising Center. During her tenure in campus activities, she expanded the student organization program, increasing the number of active student clubs by 75%. Through her role in advising, Munsch is working with colleagues to streamline the enrollment, testing, and advising process as part of a Title III grant. In addition to her workplace activities, she completed her doctorate in higher education administration from New York University. Her research interests include the experiences of undocumented college students, the transfer process as a barrier to baccalaureate completion, the relationship between remediation and involvement, and the implementation of open-access missions on community college campuses.

BETSY OUDENHOVEN is president at the Community College of Aurora in Colorado. She has over 30 years of experience in higher education and has worked at four-year public state universities in Wisconsin, Minnesota, and New York; a four-year private university in Illinois; and three different community colleges in Illinois. She received her PhD in higher education from Loyola University Chicago, her MA in counseling from the University of Colorado Boulder, and her BA in psychology from St. Lawrence University. Oudenhoven's dissertation was on Generation 1.5 Latino students and English language learning at a community college. Her article

"Remediation at the Community College: Pressing Issues, Uncertain Solutions" was published in 2002 in *Next Steps for the Community College* (Wiley, May 2002).

DANIEL J. PHELAN holds a doctor of philosophy degree in education and higher education administration from Iowa State University; a master of business administration degree from St. Ambrose University in Davenport, Iowa; and a bachelor of arts degree in business administration and an associate in arts degree from Mount St. Clare College in Clinton, Iowa. Phelan has served as president of Jackson Community College in Jackson, Michigan, since 2001, which has a residence life program located on its central campus.

SUSAN J. PROCTER earned a doctoral degree in educational leadership from Eastern Michigan University. She has a master's degree in educational media and technology from Eastern Michigan and a certificate in web-based instruction from Simon Fraser University. She is employed at Eastern Michigan as a senior instructional technologist and has over 15 years of experience in instructional design and development, web-based course development, and adult learning. Her research interests include technology literacy and the usability of online learning environments.

SUSAN SALVADOR is vice president of enrollment and student affairs at Northampton Community College in Bethlehem, Pennsylvania. She served as a contributor to *Learning Reconsidered: A Campus-wide Focus on the Student Experience* (Washington, DC: American College Personnel Association and National Association of Student Personnel Administrators, 2004), and she served on the national writing team that produced the inventory statements for the "Principles of Good Practice for Student Affairs" (Washington, DC: National Association of Student Personnel Administrators and American College Personnel Association College Student Educators International, 1997), sponsored by the American College Personnel Association and the National Association of Student Personnel Administrators. She has also written articles on the impact of and philosophical changes in residence halls at two-year colleges. Salvador served as vice president of the American College Personnel Association (2009–2010) and as president in 2010–2011. She holds a doctorate in higher education administration from the University of Michigan, a master's in student personnel and counseling from Pennsylvania State University, and a bachelor's in psychology from Siena College.

TAMARA N. STEVENSON is assistant professor in speech communication at Westminster College in Salt Lake City, Utah. Previously she served as a post-doctoral teaching fellow in speech at Westminster College. In addition, she was a visiting assistant professor in educational leadership at Miami University in Ohio. Stevenson's scholarly interests include community college leadership, critical race theory, critical communication pedagogy, social justice, and equity in higher education. Her professional background consists of more than 10 years in print and broadcast journalism and corporate communications in the automotive industry; in health care; as well as in the K–12 and two- and four-year college settings. Her work "Combat in the Academy: Racial Battle Fatigue, Role Strain, and African American Faculty at Public Community Colleges" is featured in the book *Confronting Racism in Higher Education: Problems and Possibilities for Fighting Ignorance, Bigotry and Isolation* (Charlotte, NC: Information Age, 2013).

JULIE URANIS is a doctoral candidate at Eastern Michigan University and is pursuing a certificate in distance education from the University of Wisconsin–Madison. She has a master of science in technology studies as well as a graduate certificate in community college leadership from Eastern Michigan. At Western Kentucky University she directs the distance learning and adult and continuing education units. With experience in teaching and advising adult learners, she focuses her research on community college career and technical programs and online learning.

TANIA VELAZQUEZ is a counselor at Suffolk County Community College, Michael J. Grant Campus. She sits on several collegewide committees including collegewide assessment, campus safety, and Title III grant. Tania's commitment to her students is evident in her involvement as faculty adviser for the Gay Straight Alliance. She was named Faculty Adviser of the Year in 2013. She earned her associate's degree in liberal arts at Suffolk Community College, bachelor's degree in psychology at State University of New York at Geneseo, and her master of social work degree with a specialization in student community development at Stony Brook University. She is also enrolled in the Master of Higher Education Administration Program at Stony Brook University.

JESSE S. WATSON is associate director of graduate programs for diversity outreach and academic professional development at the University of Southern California, Graduate School, Los Angeles. He received his PhD from the HALE Higher, Adult, and Lifelong Education program in the College of Education at Michigan State University. His dissertation focused on the experiences of White students who participated in monoethnic, minority, nonmulticultural groups. Additionally, his research interests include issues of equity and diversity with a focus on critical White studies, how students experience whiteness, systemic whiteness, community colleges and marginalized communities, and campus ecology. He coedited an issue of *New Directions for Community Colleges* regarding marginalized populations in community colleges.

Index

187

first generation college students, provides concrete recommendations for practice in service to this growing population of undergraduates, and, thus, brings us several steps closer to an answer."

—Jennifer R. Keup,
Director, National Resource Center for The First-Year Experience and Students in Transition

Empowering Women in Higher Education and Student Affairs
Theory, Research, Narratives, and Practice From Feminist Perspectives
Edited by Penny A. Pasque and Shelley Errington Nicholson
Foreword by Linda J. Sax

How do we interrupt the current paradigms of sexism in the academy? How do we construct a new and inclusive gender paradigm that resists the dominant values of the patriarchy? And why are these agendas important not just for women, but for higher education as a whole?

These are the questions that these extensive and rich analyses of the historical and contemporary roles of women in higher education—as administrators, faculty, students, and student affairs professionals—seek constructively to answer. In doing so they address the intersection of gender and women's other social identities, such as of race, ethnicity, sexual orientation, class, and ability.

Multicultural Student Services on Campus
Building Bridges, Re-visioning Community
Edited by Dafina Lazarus Stewart

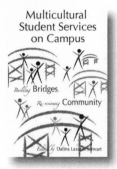

For new professionals in multicultural student services (MSS), this book constitutes a thorough introduction to the structure, organization, and scope of the services and educational mission of these units. For senior practitioners it offers insights for re-evaluating their strategies, and inspiration to explore new possibilities.

"The authors offer a collective vision of multicultural student services (MSS) that takes the best of what we have learned in the past to move forward in re-visioning the higher education community of the future. This is a bold vision of a newly-fashioned MSS that connects and integrates issues of race and ethnicity with those of sexual orientation, gender identity and religious expression, and takes MSS away from the margins of student and academic affairs units to become a key venue to assist in building transformative and democratic campus communities."

—Laura I. Rendón,
Professor at the University of Texas–San Antonio

22883 Quicksilver Drive
Sterling, VA 20166-2102   Subscribe to our e-mail alerts: www.Styluspub.com

ACPA titles available from Stylus

The Art of Effective Facilitation
Reflections From Social Justice Educators
Edited by Lisa M. Landreman

How can I apply learning and social justice theory to become a better facilitator?
Should I prepare differently for workshops around specific identities?
How do I effectively respond when things aren't going as planned?

This book is intended for the increasing number of faculty and student affairs administrators—at whatever their level of experience—who are being are asked to become social justice educators to prepare students to live successfully within, and contribute to, an equitable multicultural society.

It will enable facilitators to create programs that go beyond superficial discussion of the issues to fundamentally address the structural and cultural causes of inequity, and provide students with the knowledge and skills to work for a more just society. Beyond theory, design, techniques, and advice on practice, the book concludes with a section on supporting student social action.

Why Aren't We There Yet?
Taking Personal Responsibility for Creating an Inclusive Campus
Edited by Jan Arminio, Vasti Torres, and Raechele L. Pope

This book focuses on guiding individuals and groups through learning how to have difficult conversations that lead us to act to create more just campuses, and provides illustrations of multiple ways to respond to difficult situations. It advocates for engaging in fruitful dialogues regarding differing social identities including race, ethnicity, religion, gender, and sexual orientation, to lead readers through a process that advocates for justice, and for taking personal responsibility for contributing to the solution.

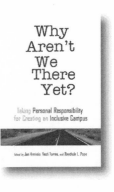

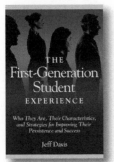

The First Generation Student Experience
Implications for Campus Practice, and Strategies for Improving Persistence and Success
Jeff Davis

"Jeff Davis does an excellent job of defining, deciphering, and discussing the experiences, issues, and successes of first generation college students on both the individual and institutional levels. However, the real richness of this resource comes from the voices of students themselves. Hearing their stories through personal narratives illustrates both the diversity of background yet the commonality of challenge that first generation college students experience in their transitions into and through higher education. The content of this book has the power to inspire higher educators to examine their commitment to the success of